# LIKE I SAY

*Len Jenkin*

**BROADWAY PLAY PUBLISHING INC**
New York
www.broadwayplaypublishing.com
info@broadwayplaypublishing.com

First published by B P P I in June 1999 in the collection
*Plays By Len Jenkin*
First printing, this edition: December 2013
I S B N: 978-0-88145-412-3

Book design: Marie Donovan
Page make-up: Adobe Indesign
Typeface: Palatino
Printed and bound in the U S A

## ABOUT THE AUTHOR

Len Jenkin's plays include DARK RIDE, TIME IN
KAFKA, AMERICAN NOTES, PILGRIMS OF THE
NIGHT, CARELESS LOVE, MY UNCLE SAM, LIMBO
TALES, PSALM 151, and LIKE I SAY. His works for
the stage, often directed by him, have been produced
throughout the United States, as well as in England,
France, Denmark, Germany and Japan. His adaptations
for the stage include Voltaire's CANDIDE (Guthrie
Theater, Minneapolis), Aristophanes' THE BIRDS
(Yale Repertory Theater, New Haven), and Kafka's A
COUNTRY DOCTOR (Classic Stage Company, New
York).

His novel *N Judah* is currently available in bookstores
and on the web at lenjenkin.com. He has also worked
in television and for feature films.

He has received three OBIE awards for Directing and
Playwriting, a Guggenheim Fellowship, a Rockefeller
Foundation Award, a nomination for an Emmy
Award, the Helen Merrill Award, and four National
Endowment for the Arts Fellowships.

He teaches in the Dramatic Writing Department, Tisch
School of the Arts, New York University.

LIKE I SAY was first produced by the Flea Theater in New York (Jim Simpson and Carol Ostrow, Producers) in the Fall of 2003. The cast and creative contributors were:

Oberson Adjepong
Paula Ehrenburg
Matt Dellapina
Fernando Gambaroni
Shari Hellman
Lanna Joffrey
Caroline Messihi
Melissa Miller
Jerry Nauman
Jack O'Neill
John Peterson
Jonathan Phillips
Sayra Player
Jerry Zellers

*Director* ............................................................. Len Jenkin
*Set design, puppet theatre design, props &*
*puppets* ................................................................. Sue Rees
*Lighting* ............................................................. Andrew Hill
*Sound design* ..................................................... John Kilgore

# CHARACTERS

*At the Hotel Splendide:*

ISAIAH SANDOVAL, *a dreamer*
ROSE, *his caretaker*
LITTLE JUNIOR, *a hotel employee*
HELENA SKATE, *a hotel manager*
MR HAROLD SCHWARZBERG, *an artist*
LEON VOLE, *a traveling puppeteer*
TANYA VOLE, *another traveling puppeteer*

*and, with* COCONUT JOE:

*In America:*
COCONUT JOE ISKOWITZ
*his* DAUGHTER
PRESIDENT ARTHUR KRUMM

*In Germany:*
BARON DRAMER
INGA
AVA
NANCY
M C
POLICE

*In the mountains:*
ANTIRADIATION SUIT
FOREMAN
GUARDS
RAGGEDY MAN

WEALTHY SPA GUESTS
DOCTOR MOTO

*In Venice, Italy:*
MASKED VENETIANS
CONTESSA
FRIEDA
COUNT ORSINO
OPERA SINGERS

*At sea:*
CAPTAIN NIK-NIK
TARTAR SAILORS
PIRATES
PIRATE QUEEN *(AVA)*

*On the island:*
ISLANDERS
MR WHELK
DIEUDONNE


LIKE I SAY *requires a minimum of eight actors if all the
roles in the "Coconut Joe" sections, except* COCONUT
JOE *himself, are doubled by the performers in the "Hotel
Splendide" sections. The play can also be performed with
more than eight, using an additional group of actors to play
all the roles in "Coconut Joe".*

This play is for Beatrice Jenkin, who, late in life, came a very long way to see it, and had a wonderful time.

# ACT ONE

*(The Hotel Splendide—somewhere on the coast of the
United States. Once a grand hotel, the place is now a barely
habitable wreck. Huge public rooms have gone to seed.
Peeling paint, exposed wiring, trash piled in corners.)*

*(The hotel is still functioning, however desperately. Here at
the very tip of the peninsula, the power is unreliable, and the
lights flicker.)*

## PART ONE
### In The Garden

*(A walled garden, behind the hotel. It's early spring, nothing
yet in bud or flower. There's an arched doorway in one wall,
leading to a rocky shoreline of cliffs, overlooking the ocean.
Another door leads into the hotel.)*

*(The stone walls of the garden are partially draped in  canvas
drop-cloths. A ladder, some buckets of paint. Someone is
painting the garden walls, but the results of that labor can't
be seen. Lawn furniture, and some indoor furniture that has
been left outside for a few seasons. A phone. Chinese lanterns
hang overhead, unlit.)*

*(Somewhere, not too far away, the sea)*

## Scene One

*(In the garden)*

*(MR SCHWARZBERG is tattooing ROSE's back. Intermittent buzz of the tattoo machine.)*

*(ROSE is in her early twenties. SCHWARZBERG is mid-sixties. His face is disfigured by heavy scarring, as if from a terrible burn sustained long ago.)*

*(ISAIAH is a man of indeterminate age. He can seem youthful and energetic, and the next moment confused and broken. Now he's seated in the garden with his back to us, smoking a cigarette.)*

ISAIAH: A cigarette is burning. Smoke rises from a green glass ashtray. Green glass ashtray, smoke sails up into the light.
Wait here, right here. And we'll begin.
Now.
In the beginning, the Hotel Splendide was built, in the chaos of ice and the polar... No. Take it downtown, on the Boulevard des Singes, Calle del Morto, Azalea Avenue by the sea.
*(Sings)* By the sea, by the sea,
By the beautiful sea
You and me, you and me
Oh how happy we'll be...
All right. On Azalea Avenue by the Sonic Drive-In, girl in a white dress boards a tram, blue sparks, and a little bell rings...
Put it in the backyard. A to Z Cash Pawn, Plutonium Road, Pee-Wee's Kampus Kitchen, El Sombrero's Sirloin Stockade.
Think about it, cowgirl.
A single raindrop ripples the dead canal, sets the black boat rocking. She's naked in the gondola, Pall Malls spilled over the red plush seat. The pupils of her eyes

are huge. The lantern sways, and his shadow dances
a dumb, jerky dance. The darkness is deep, black, and
forever. Their bodies are wonderful, invisible things…
Sail away, sail away, sail away…
Empty highway, body in a ditch, little wind comes
up…

ROSE: Isaiah, when are we leaving?

ISAIAH: When I'm well enough. No miracles have
occurred, Rose. Not yet.

ROSE: (*Chanting*) We're here because we're here
because we're here because we're here, we're here
because we're…

ISAIAH: Shut up.

ROSE: I'm in with the fucking zombies here. Zombies
by the sea.

SCHWARZBERG: Hold still.

ROSE: Mister S, you got a cigarette?

SCHWARZBERG: Young girls shouldn't smoke. It's no
good for them. Besides, my cigarettes—it's Luckies.

(SCHWARZBERG *hands* ROSE *the pack. She takes one, lights
up.*)

ROSE: You know why we didn't get our check this
month?

ISAIAH: No, and I'm not interested in thinking about it.

ROSE: I think, Isaiah, that your family has decided to
give up on you. They believe you get me from the
escort service, and you're throwing the rest of your
allowance into the sea.

ISAIAH: Is that the way for a nurse to talk to a delicate
patient?

ROSE: I'm no nurse, Isaiah. If you want a nurse, get
yourself one. You know, I'm supposed to see you don't

get into any trouble, but you haven't wandered off too far for a month now, and when you do I can tell you want me to find you. Oooooh, you know what, Isaiah? I figure you love me. Zat true?

SCHWARZBERG: Hold still, Rosie.

ROSE: Zat it?

ISAIAH: Yes, actually.

ROSE: I thought so.

ISAIAH: Or maybe I'm tired. I've been unhappy for so long—it's a lot of work, Rose, this kind of misery.

ROSE: You're better. I quit.

ISAIAH: You can't go, Rosie. I'm gonna need my muse. Someday. Maybe.

ROSE: You be *my* little muse, Isaiah. Then I'll stay.

ISAIAH: Come on, Rose. You have no money, no place to go, and a boyfriend looking to carve his initials in your neck.

SCHWARZBERG: The two of you put together don't know shit about anything. Stop wiggling, you're making me sloppy. I haven't done this kind of work in ten years. If you hadn't found my old tattoo box in the shed...

ROSE: I knew you were an artiste, Mister S. I just didn't know you did skin.

SCHWARZBERG: I'm all kinds of a professor, little darling.

*(A silence. Buzz of the tattoo needle)*

ISAIAH: What'd you get, Rose?

ROSE: None of your business.

ISAIAH: Mister Schwarzberg, give me a break here. It's the Roadrunner. Beep! Beep! BEEP!

ROSE: Isaiah. Please.

SCHWARZBERG: What goes on your body, that's private business. If Rose wants you to know her business, she'll tell you her business.

(LITTLE JUNIOR *enters, early twenties, work clothes. His pants legs and shoes are wet. He watches* SCHWARZBERG *at work on* ROSE's *bare back.*)

(*The buzzing stops.*)

SCHWARZBERG: Done. I can't guarantee that one more than ten days after you're buried. Keep it out from under freight trains.

(SCHWARZBERG *tapes a piece of gauze over the tattoo.* ROSE *stands, slips on her shirt. She looks over at* LITTLE JUNIOR.)

ROSE: Hey, Little Junior. Where you been?

LITTLE JUNIOR: Down on the cliffs.

(*Silence. Sound of the sea*)

(LITTLE JUNIOR *begins some work in the garden.*)

ISAIAH: Indiana, and out by Gary the stacks are on fire, night of stars through the black smoke… I gotta see a man. I gotta see a man in Kokomo. All right. Tract house by a liverwurst sandwich. Cheerios. Ding-dong. Gotta go, honey. Go straight to school. Miss Jefferson'll pick you up. Gotta go. Gotta go-go… He's got a beautiful daughter and a heart of gold, and a wife in the ditch, black water in her nostrils… Empty highway, body in a ditch, little wind comes up…

## Scene Two

(*Same garden, later*)

(HELENA, *attractive, late twenties, casual dress—the hotel manager. She's with* LEON *and* TANYA VOLE, *prospective guests. The* VOLES, *late thirties to early forties, are theatrical and exotic— "foreign" in a hard-to-define way. They look as if they've seen better days.)*

LEON: Nice dewy place you have here.

HELENA: We're at the tip of the peninsula. Surrounded on three sides by the sea. You can't really get any further east...

LEON: A blessed haven—in an increasingly disturbing and erratic world.

HELENA: Glad you like it. Uh, how long do you...

LEON: Do you realize the dark ages are again upon us? The difficulties that beset commercial travelers are legion. Trains are infrequent, accommodations wretched, and roadside prostitutes will murder you right there in the sawgrass and roll you into a drainage ditch. No respect for the clientele.

*(Silence. Sound of the sea)*

LEON: Very still, isn't it? No one else was on our train. No other cars were moving but the one you sent down to the station for us.

TANYA: Some kind of plague...

LEON: No other people for miles.

TANYA: It's difficult to survive as a performing artist if your audience is dead.

HELENA: It's true. We are the last human beings. I heard it on the news.

LEON: There's no need to mock of my wife. Tanya hasn't been well. Something in the lungs. We'll need to impose on your generosity for a few days. We are expecting a payment...

TANYA: From our last engagement. Our booking agent is...

*(Phone rings.* HELENA *picks up.)*

HELENA: Uh, Mister Whelk?… Fine. Uh, how're things in Bimini?… You did? It'll look great in the ballroom… The ad is running all the time. Constantly. It's perpetual… Yeah… Uh, *(Looking at the* VOLES*)* business has picked up. Doubled. But there's still the matter of the wiring. And we had some storm damage over the winter… Little Junior's not here right now, but I can tell you there's no way him and Mister Schwarzberg can make the kind of repairs we need out of scrap lumber and roofing tin…I'll tell him. I'll tell him, but unless you… Yeah. Bye. *(Hangs up)* Fuck you. *(To* VOLES*)* Sorry for the interruption. How long will you be staying?

TANYA: Indefinitely.

LEON: Forever.

TANYA: A little joke. We need to rest, recuperate. Our performing schedule has been quite heavy.

HELENA: What sort of performing do you do, exactly?

LEON: We are puppeteers. The Vole Family Puppet Theater. We offer entertainments for children or adults. Fairs, schools, private parties. We've been touring the United States. Tanya Vole, Queen of Magic, performer for this theater.

*(*TANYA *bows.)*

LEON: Leon Vole, author and creator of the mise-en-scène. *(He bows.)* Some of our bookings have been erratic. In fact, our agent seems to have had his phone disconnected.

TANYA: Temporarily, Leon.

LEON: In any case, we're here. This hotel comes highly recommended.

HELENA: Really? By who?

TANYA: Friends—of friends.

LEON: A charming couple. He had a severe limp. I can't recall his name at the moment. They did say a friend of theirs was staying here—Isaiah Sandoval.

HELENA: I'll have to check the guest book.

TANYA: It must be difficult recalling, when you have so many guests.

HELENA: What do you want with him?

LEON: We heard he was good company. A writer. It's difficult to find clever conversation on the edge of the world.

HELENA: I'll need a week's rent when your funds arrive. Soon, I hope.

(LITTLE JUNIOR *enters, carrying parts of a large puppet theater broken down to wood and canvas. He puts them down, exits.*)

HELENA: By the way, the accommodations aren't all they might be. You see, repairs are…

TANYA: Please. Say no more. Once, we had to walk from the Red Gates to Novodevichie Monastery in a snowstorm, with the entire theatre on our backs.

LEON: Twenty miles!

TANYA: We spent seven months among the distant villages in Volokolamski Province—

LEON: Russkov and Moshaiska!

TANYA: We slept in the puppet booth. Our covers were the threadbare show curtains. I would lay my head on the little mattresses from The Princess and the Pea…

LEON: While we were performing one day, a large, white pig came into our booth from the rear. It calmly looked around and calmly walked out again.

HELENA: Really? Well, I'll get the room ready. It'll only be a moment…

LEON: Are you married?

(LITTLE JUNIOR *enters, carrying the rest of the* VOLES'*s gear—the remainder of the puppet theater, props, boxes, and a rat cage with a live rat.)*

TANYA: Ah! Our puppet theater.

LITTLE JUNIOR: Helena, where does this stuff…?

LEON: And an added attraction, the Dancing Rat. The waltz. A passionate tango. Something to amuse the parents while the children watch Puss and Boots.

HELENA: You travel with a rat?

LEON: The most talented member of our troupe. After Miss Tanya. His name is Boris Tomaschevsky.

HELENA: I don't believe this.

TANYA: We are not a dream of yours, Miss…

HELENA: Skate. Helena Skate.

TANYA: We are all too real, Miss Skate. A theater like ours is simply no longer common.

LEON: Indeed. The fucking cinema and fucking television have made some inroads into the profession.

TANYA: *(Uncovering the rat's cage)* Ah, there he is. Unaccustomed to the light. Hello, Marlon.

HELENA: I thought the rat was…

LEON: Marlon, Sir Laurence, or Boris Tomaschevsky. Depending on the clientele.

TANYA: Actually, he's a lady. A dancing rat lady.

HELENA: Little Junior, put the theater in the ballroom. Give them some old vegetables for the rat, and show them their room. Drinks are out here at twilight, if the weather holds.

LEON: I'm sure it will.

TANYA: Lead on, Little Junior. Take us to our room. I need a bath.

## Scene Three

*(Same garden, even later)*

*(Some of the dropcloths covering the garden wall are gone. SCHWARZBERG, up on a ladder, drops another. On the wall is an extraordinary painting, garish and frightening. We can see some of it, though portions are still concealed. Parts are weathered, and parts look new, as if the artist has been working on it, off and on, for years.)*

*(It is an American Dance of Death on the garden wall: a series of images of those surprised and led away by Death—a dancing, grinning skeleton. Each image contains Death— and a politician, a movie star, a scientist, young child, old woman, etc. Each scene is separate, and yet all are linked in a strange parade around the garden wall.)*

*(SCHWARZBERG has paints and brushes with him on the ladder. He paints.)*

*(ROSE watches.)*

ROSE: Mister S, how can you think about death so much?

SCHWARZBERG: It's my job. I hired myself. God's painter. This garden is my synagogue.

ROSE: Your spookhouse. You think God wants us to be frightened? These things are scary.

SCHWARZBERG: Not to me. My alarm clock, wake everybody up. One eye sees death over your shoulder, maybe you live life better.

ROSE: We need a reminder that we're gonna die? Even I know that much.

SCHWARZBERG: *(Chanting)* Pray for the dead
And the dead will pray for you
That's just because
They have nothing else to do
The original painting was in the Church of the Holy
Innocents, in the Old World, on the wall around
the church cemetery. Now that wall is gone, the
cemetery is gone, the church is gone. There's a city
housing project there now. I'm making a modern
update. Streamline. A money in your asspocket tourist
attraction.

ROSE: And a word to the wise.

*(LITTLE JUNIOR enters. His shoes and pantslegs are wet, as he's been tromping about the cliffs and tide pools. He holds up a pair of baggy pants.)*

LITTLE JUNIOR: Mister S, some raccoon must have
pulled your pants outta your room. I found them on
the cliff.

SCHWARZBERG: Crackers. I keep saltines in my pockets.
Raccoons like them.

LITTLE JUNIOR: The animals are starting to cross the line
around here. They can't tell the difference between this
place and their natural habitat.

ROSE: It's all right with me. Let the grizzly bears dance
in the ballroom.

LITTLE JUNIOR: It's not gonna be all right with Helena.
All she needs is for Mister Whelk to show up, find
raccoon shit in the hallway. You, uh, going to town
later?

ROSE: If Isaiah seems cool. Maybe.

LITTLE JUNIOR: Maybe?

ROSE: Yeah. May be.

LITTLE JUNIOR: If you do go into town, and I realize you're not saying you will, but maybe, but if it should fall out that you do, would you like to shoot some pool? With me? I go to McRory's, which is a family place with a snackbar.

ROSE: You play nine-ball?

LITTLE JUNIOR: Nine-ball?

ROSE: You going deaf? From being out on the cliffs, with no one around?

LITTLE JUNIOR: No. I just don't know what…

ROSE: I don't mind that you like me, Little Junior, but it's getting old.

(SCHWARZBERG *comes down from his ladder.*)

SCHWARZBERG: Compliments. You got to say beautiful things to women. I was a great loverboy, before my face became a mess. *(To* ROSE*)* Little darling, you look as stylish as a white goose under a red wagon.

(ROSE *laughs.*)

LITTLE JUNIOR: You know, Mister S, with the tourist season coming, Helena's gonna ask me to whitewash these walls, hang some Christmas lights.

SCHWARZBERG: And you would do it? You'd follow orders, ten years' work and you would whitewash? The Nazi Tom Sawyer.

LITTLE JUNIOR: I'm just telling you. She might ask me.

SCHWARZBERG: I'll call Mister Whelk himself. I know the number. You think I don't know Mister Whelk? I got the number in Bimini.

LITTLE JUNIOR: That number's written on the wall next to the pay phone.

SCHWARZBERG: I was a dishwasher and a drunk. A mean drunk, working a crowded shift. I fell into the

Fryolator. Tssss! When I was covered with bandages, Mister Whelk came to the hospital. He was the only visitor I had. He said, "Stay at the Hotel Splendide as long as you like, my friend".

LITTLE JUNIOR: Mister Whelk still wants this place to make money.

SCHWARZBERG: That's why he's gonna love this. Say you go see the Mona Lisa. Five bucks, and she's enigmatic. Here you get great art and a message.

LITTLE JUNIOR: What message?

SCHWARZBERG: Don't fall into the Fryolator.

ROSE: Come on, Mister Schwarzberg.

SCHWARZBERG: O K. Ashes to ashes, dust to dust— show me a woman that a man can trust. *(He turns to go.)* Nooze or Mirra, Nooze. Nooze or Mirra, Nooze…

*(Silence. ROSE and LITTLE JUNIOR look at each other.)*

## Scene Four

*(Same garden. Twilight)*

*(Some of the Chinese lanterns are lit. SCHWARZBERG has left a floodlight on a portion of the painting he's been working on, high on the wall.)*

*(HELENA has set out a tray of drinks, snacks. LITTLE JUNIOR has an old waiter's jacket on and serves. ROSE brings ISAIAH a drink, sits near him. HELENA and SCHWARZBERG talk quietly. TANYA approaches ISAIAH and ROSE.)*

TANYA: Isaiah Sandoval. I've read your books. All of them.

ISAIAH: Do you want something from me?

TANYA: I haven't decided yet.

ISAIAH: Did you like the books?

TANYA: Yes, in a way. Sour, pretentious, sentimental—
some of my favorite qualities.

ROSE: Lady, you don't know what the fuck you're
talking about.

ISAIAH: Quiet, Rose. At last there's a critic I can agree
with.

TANYA: You'd like to be an artist, but you haven't got
the balls for it, Mister Sandoval. Or the heart.

HELENA: You're wrong, Mrs Vole. I read with great
care, and I'm just as clever as the next girl. Isaiah, your
books are pretty wonderful, and I'm not saying this to
hear myself talk.

ISAIAH: Those books were written ten years ago. Before
I knew how…

ROSE: Isaiah, please. Not that shit.

ISAIAH: All right. I'll behave myself. Helena, I am
thrilled, delighted, and fucking surprised. Those stories
full of lies and horseshit actually meant something to
you.

HELENA: You heard me. And you won't change my
mind.

ISAIAH: Well, well. Fame. Even the landlady reads your
stuff.

HELENA: Only since you got here. I was curious about
you. The bookstore in town special ordered them for
me.

ISAIAH: Special order. It's a Sandoval revival, and I'm
not even dead yet. Rose, you got my medicine?

ROSE: Yeah, I…

ISAIAH: Throw it into the sea. Let the sharks gobble
them up. Calm sharks. Cheerful.

ROSE: Actually, you need to take one about now. And no more alcohol.

(ROSE *shakes a pill out of a bottle. She gives the pill to* ISAIAH. *He takes it, reluctantly, with a swallow of his drink.*)

TANYA: You know, Mister Sandoval, I was teasing you. I haven't read your books at all. Perhaps I will, someday. I'm an artist myself. So is my husband.

ISAIAH: Helena, collect in advance from Mrs Vole. She's an artist in America.

TANYA: You know, Rose, it might have been a special friend of yours who suggested this hotel to us. A place to take it easy, he said.

ROSE: Eddie? Was his name...

TANYA: Eddie? I don't remember.

ROSE: You get to know him?

TANYA: Fairly well.

(*A silence*)

HELENA: Mrs Vole, where's your husband?

TANYA: He took a walk along the cliffs. He's a great lover of nature in its darker moods—rough seas, storms, lightning.

SCHWARZBERG: He's wasting his time. It's a calm night. But there should be a crescent moon over the sea. Lover's moon. (*He howls like a wolf.*) Aaoooooo! Ahooooo!!

LITTLE JUNIOR: Mrs Vole, could you...tell us about the puppets.

TANYA: The Vole Family Puppet Theater. I won't bore you with the full history, which goes back seven generations. Enough to say that Leon's father was a puppeteer. He left him the theater, taught him. Do you want to meet the cast?

ROSE: Cast of what?

TANYA: *The Crystal Castle.* One moment, and I'll bring them out and introduce you.

(TANYA *goes inside. Quiet. Sound of the sea*)

HELENA: You did good work today, Rose. Maybe tomorrow, you can start on cleaning out that ballroom. The trash gets hauled on Wednesday, so…

ISAIAH: What are you talking about?

HELENA: You owe me money. You don't have any. So I asked Rose to give me a hand.

ISAIAH: Rose is not a chambermaid.

HELENA: Oh. And I am. I'm the chambermaid, and Rose is the Queen of Sheba.

ROSE: Isaiah, I can help us out. I'm living here too, you know.

HELENA: I'm trying to be nice here. I got to pay Little Junior, and I got bills. I take that out of income, of which there isn't any. Hell of a job, but it's all I've got. At least there's a leaky roof over my head. So, even though you're two months behind, I won't kick you out—today. I'll check with Mister Whelk, but I know what he'll say—cash better appear, and soon. Meanwhile, Rose has gotta help around here, and I'll ask you too, Isaiah, as soon as you're able. You can make my bed.

(TANYA *returns, carrying a large cardboard box full of puppets.*)

TANYA: The company of *The Crystal Castle of Kindness.* Our current offering for the tots. One of the most ancient and beautiful tales of all. Leon wrote it last month. They weren't coming to our Puss and Boots, though this didn't do much better. *(She shows the puppet cast of The Crystal Castle to the group, one by one. Each is displayed with some clever manipulation on her hand, and a final bow by the puppet.)* The Princess. The Siamese Twins. The Duke. His Lawyers. Ah! Here's the Hangman. And the Hangman's Beautiful Daughter. The Devil. And his Crocodile.

*(The crocodile puppet lunges suddenly at* TANYA's *throat. She hauls him off herself, after some difficulty, with a flourish.)*

*(The group applauds.)*

TANYA: Thank you. The theater of live actors is a pale imitation of life. Only these simple puppets capture the soul in their unchanging faces. Every puppet taking part in our performances deserves to be called a living being.

ISAIAH: Living beings. Little breeze comes up in Indiana, old newspaper blows down a back street, and the puppets are dancing…
Fuck yes. It's him.
It's Coconut Joe, coming at you courtesy of the international dateline and the robin's egg, hatching out in a blue serge suit and a fifty-cent necktie. Mrs Vole, allow me to return the favor. Mister Schwarzberg, sing me that song I like…
SCHWARZBERG: *(Sings)*
Oh the humming of the bees in the cigarette trees
By the soda wa…crystal water fountain
Whiskey springs where the bluebird sings…
In the Big Rock Candy Mountain
In the Big Rock Candy Mountain
There's a land that's fair and bright…

ISAIAH: Coconut Joe, Mister U S A, a hard-working son of a bitch, put on your suit, comb your hair, make the kid lunch, drop her at school, go to the office say, "Hiya, Mabel", and get to work.

The story of Coconut Joe. Part One.

*(Crossfade: The story of Coconut Joe, Part One)*

*(Music.* COCONUT JOE *appears.)*

COCONUT JOE: Hi, everybody, I'm Coconut Joe, known from Maine to Mexico! The coconut man from Kokomo! Joseph Iskowitz, the coconut buyer for Universal Bake Shoppe, a multi-national corporation, shipping with love from Indiana to the world. I have a dead wife and a live daughter, age ten.

*(Phone rings. In another space, a posh office with* PRESIDENT ARTHUR KRUMM *of Universal Bake Shoppe on the other end of the line)*

COCONUT JOE: Coconut Joe here.

PHONE VOICE: Listen, Joe. This is Arthur Krumm.

COCONUT JOE: Who? I don't believe I know...

KRUMM: President Krumm. The president of Universal Bake Shoppe. Your boss, you idiot.

COCONUT JOE: Sorry, Mister Krumm sir.

KRUMM: Joe, we're in trouble here at Universal. I miscalculated on some investments. We're depending on the new Coconut Dee-Lite Cookie to save the company from bankruptcy. We need to buy a thousand tons of coconut. I want you to make the buy through a friend of mine, Baron Hans Dramer at the Berlin Produce Exchange, Berlin, Germany. He's a dealer in the finest desiccated flake.

COCONUT JOE: But, boss, I've never even been to Europe. I don't know the language. I...

KRUMM: It's a cash transaction, Joe. Pick up the bag of money at my office. And your plane ticket. You leave tonight.

ISAIAH: Joe went home to his little daughter and told her all about it. They got a picture book of the Old World and looked through it together after dinner...

*(COCONUT JOE's DAUGHTER, age ten, breaks into tears.)*

COCONUT JOE: Honey, don't you worry. Mrs Jefferson will be staying with you.

*(Her sobs increase.)*

DAUGHTER: You're never coming back, Daddy. Never never never.

*(They embrace.)*

COCONUT JOE: That's not true, honey. You know I love you so much. Let's see that smile. *(Sings)* Oooh the buzzing of the bees in the cigarette trees... *(She joins in.)*

DAUGHTER & COCONUT JOE: *(Sing)*
...beside the crystal fountain
Come with me and we'll go see
The Big Rock Candy Mountain.

COCONUT JOE: I have to go. I'll be back in just seven days.

*(COCONUT JOE goes. His DAUGHTER breaks into tears again.)*

ISAIAH: Coconut Joe boards a plane.

LUFTHANSA STEWARDESS: Welcome to Berlin. Get off the plane.

*(Music and sound. Berlin. The Produce Exchange)*

ISAIAH: The Produce Exchange in Berlin. Joe meets the Syndic of the Exchange, hereditary Knight of Westphalia, Chief of Coconut Importation, friend of President Krumm of Universal Bake Shoppe—Baron Hans Joachim Dramer.

DRAMER: Ah, Herr Iskowitz. Come in, come in. Take Herr Iskowitz's coat, Inga. That's a good girl. Walk this way, my dear Herr Iskowitz.

*(They walk this way.)*

DRAMER: This way, my American friend. To the coconut.

ISAIAH: On they went, these two lovers of coconut, to the inner chamber of the... No. They are actually in a fucked-up warehouse down by the Berlin docks. Dramer rips open a burlap sack, takes out a coconut.

DRAMER: A particularly potent shipment of Filipino nuts got in this morning, transshipped via Antwerp.

COCONUT JOE: Palawan? Mindanao?

*(Ethereal coconut music)*

DRAMER: Zamboanga Angel Food—the purest of the pure—like mountain snow. May I crack you one?

*(BARON DRAMER takes a machete out of nowhere and dehusks, slices, and dices a coconut before our eyes. He puts the results on a silver tray.)*

ISAIAH: Joe sniffs...
Joe tastes!

COCONUT JOE: Baron, this is the most wonderful coconut I have ever...

DRAMER: Say no more. The Coconut Dee-Lite Cookie will sweep the world. Do we have a deal?

COCONUT JOE: I'll say!
Here's our payment in full.

*(COCONUT JOE hands DRAMER the bag of money.)*

COCONUT JOE: I'll come around tomorrow morning and make sure every sack of nuts comes up to our specs, but with Zamboanga Angel Food I'm sure there'll be no problem.

DRAMER: Of course not. You'll also need to arrange shipping, out of Venice to New York.

COCONUT JOE: Great. I'll take a train down to Venice, supervise the loading, and then it's back home to the U S A.

DRAMER: Perhaps you'd agree to have dinner tonight with me and my daughter—to celebrate.

COCONUT JOE: Wonderful! I have a daughter myself, you know. Ten years old.

DRAMER: Meet us at the Club America, in the Bundesstrasse. You'll feel right at home.

M C: Club America.

*(The* M C *is a German in a tuxedo and a cowboy hat.)*

M C: Damen und Herren, Fraulein Nancy, from the Wild Wild West! Nancy!

*(*NANCY *struts onto the stage in cowboy boots, a lariat, and not too much else—a golden-haired American girl. Go-go music.* NANCY *dances.)*

ISAIAH: Coconut Joe arrives. At his table, a very attractive young woman. Her name is Ava.

AVA: My father, Baron Dramer, couldn't be here. A sudden business emergency. Let's carry on without him. I'll do my best to amuse you…

ISAIAH: Ava Dramer lures Coconut Joe to a romantic spot, Kanalside.

AVA: Isn't this a romantic spot, Kanalside?

ISAIAH: They kiss. Grope. She unbuckles his belt…

*(*COCONUT JOE's *pants drop around his ankles.)*

ISAIAH: Who's that in the trees? Baron Dramer! And President Arthur Krumm! They wear tuxedos. They carry nine-irons. They smash Coconut Joe over the head, repeatedly, until he falls to the ground.

(COCONUT JOE *lies there.* DRAMER, KRUMM, *and* AVA *change his clothes to those of a bum.* DRAMER *pays off* AVA, *with a bag of money.)*

AVA: I kind of liked him. I never met a man that... stupid.

DRAMER: Naive is the word you're groping for, Ava. But no one is paying you for your feelings. Get lost.

KRUMM: Perhaps we could get together later, at my hotel. I'm Arthur Krumm, President of Universal Bake Shoppe, and I might have a cookie for...

AVA: Go fuck yourself. *(She's gone.)*

ISAIAH: These distinguished men of business roll the corpse of Coconut Joe into the Kanal.

*(They do so [Splash!] and disappear. Silence)*

*(Burbling and gurgling!)*

ISAIAH: He's ALIVE!

(AVA *rushes back, and hauls the bloody, groggy,* COCONUT JOE *out of the Kanal. She pumps his chest. A fountain of water from his mouth soaks them both.* COCONUT JOE *splutters, sits up.)*

COCONUT JOE: Those bastards! Owww! My head! Who hit me?

AVA: Not a clue.

COCONUT JOE: Bastards. I'm going to the police! They have laws in this... Hey, what happened to my clothes? I look like a bum.

AVA: I wouldn't go to the police, if I were you. *(She kisses him.)* I've gotta run. See you again sometime, Mister Coconut Joe.

ISAIAH: Ava, if that's her name, disappears. Joe staggers to his feet.

COP: *POLIZEI!*

*(Suddenly a flashlight beam is shining in* COCONUT JOE'*s eyes. He squints…)*

COP: POLICE!

COCONUT JOE: Cops! Am I glad to find…

COP: Silenz, Schwein. You're a lucky man. A homeless vagabond—you will soon be transformed into a hero of industry. Grab him.

*(*POLICE *throw a sack over* COCONUT JOE'*s head and haul him away.)*

COCONUT JOE: *(From under sack)* Help! I'm an American! Universal Bake Shoppe! I'm innocent! I'm… Hey! Help! HELP!

*(Sound of mountain winds. Flicker of light snow. The police are gone.* COCONUT JOE *pokes his head out of the sack. He climbs out. A* RAGGEDY MAN *is alongside him. A man completely concealed in a protective* ANTIRADIATION SUIT *is nearby.)*

ISAIAH: Where's Coconut Joe? In southern Germany, in the high mountains near the Italian border, with a herd of convicts, rapists, murderers, and homeless men. Their job? To dig a hole and bury radioactive waste.

COCONUT JOE: Oh, shit.

ANTIRADIATION SUIT: DIRTBAGS! How lucky you are to be serving the nuclear power needs of the people of Europe, and the world. Radiation levels in the spent fuel rods are monitored carefully. Your safety is our primary concern. The mountain wildlife are also our concern. They are unaffected by current radiation levels.

*(A glowing snow goose falls dead from the sky, right at* COCONUT JOE'*s feet.)*

*(And another)*

COCONUT JOE: Man, this is the deep back end of bad luck.

ISAIAH: Back end of bad luck. You like that, Rose?

ROSE: Yeah, Isaiah. I like that just fine.

*(Crossfade back to Hotel Splendide garden)*

*(The arched door leading to the cliffs is open, and standing in it is* LEON. *He has been listening very attentively. Still in the garden are* ISAIAH, ROSE, TANYA, HELENA, SCHWARZBERG, *and* LITTLE JUNIOR *in his waiter outfit.)*

LEON: *(Applauding solemnly)* Bravo. Bravo.

*(*LITTLE JUNIOR *gathers up the bottles and glasses on a tray.)*

LITTLE JUNIOR: Anybody for another drink, before I take this stuff inside...?

## Scene Five

*(The garden, early evening)*

*(All the Chinese lanterns are lit, and more of* SCHWARZBERG's *dropcloths have been taken down. The skeletons and Americans, painted, partly painted, or barely sketched in, are hard to see in the gathering darkness. The lanterns sway a bit in the breeze...)*

*(*TANYA *sits near* ISAIAH, *who is very still.)*

*(*HELENA *and* SCHWARZBERG *are drinking at a table.)*

HELENA: *(Sings)*
Once upon a time, a duck drank wine
The monkey played the fiddle on a streetcar line
The streetcar broke, the monkey choked
Trying to get to heaven on a billy goat...
That's all I remember.

SCHWARZBERG: You know, when I came here I was an alcoholic. I'd been all over the world. Everywhere I went I had less money than the place before: Buenos Aires, Mexico City, London, then New York. I always planned to make something of myself somehow and return home with rimbells on my sombrero. At one point I realized I no longer knew where home was exactly. You still got that picture of you I painted. The nude.

HELENA: Got it? It's hanging in my bedroom. I look at it and think how kind you are.

SCHWARZBERG: Kind? That painting is the truth. You were beautiful, like a guiding angel with huge feathery wings. Like a big seagull.

HELENA: Good for me.

Another drink? Little Junior!

*(He doesn't appear.)*

HELENA: Probably off on the cliffs, poking at starfish in the tide pools.

SCHWARZBERG: It's almost night. How can he see in tide pools?

HELENA: He brings a flashlight.

*(HELENA gets another drink for herself and SCHWARZBERG. They drink, quietly.)*

*(TANYA approaches ISAIAH.)*

TANYA: You're not feeling very well, are you?

ISAIAH: Can you see the North Star?

TANYA: No. No stars at all. It's overcast. Only a glow, from where the moon is behind the clouds.

ISAIAH: Who are you?

TANYA: I'm Tanya. Remember? I came here with my theatre.

ISAIAH: The hangman's beautiful daughter. I'm going inside now. Here's a candle to light you to… *(Calling)* Rose? Where's Rose?

TANYA: Rose isn't here now. She went off somewhere.

ISAIAH: She wouldn't do that

TANYA: Don't worry about Rose. I'll take you in.

ISAIAH: I don't need any help. Goodnight.

*(ISAIAH walks, a bit unsteadily, into the hotel. In a moment, TANYA gets up, goes to the arched doorway and looks out toward the cliffs and the sea. Then she steps through the doorway, disappears into darkness.)*

*(SCHWARZBERG is slumped over the table. HELENA turns on some music. She begins to dance with herself. He looks up, then rises, inspired by the tune. He dances with her.)*

*(Lights fade on the looming paintings on the garden walls. Music and sound of surf. They dance on into the darkness.)*

*(End PART ONE)*

## PART TWO

*(In the hotel—night)*

*(The grand ballroom of the Hotel Splendide—the decaying wreck of a once-great room, dust, debris. An enormous crystal chandelier hangs by two dangerously frayed wires and occasionally flickers, in tune with an erratic power supply or bad wiring.)*

*(Some stray furniture is gathered together—an old velvet sofa, a wooden crate, some odd chairs. A large window at the rear looks out on darkness.)*

## Scene One

*(In the ballroom)*

*(It's two A M, but* TANYA *and* LEON *are busy.* LEON *is setting up the puppet booth, with its striped canvas covering.* TANYA *feeds the rat through the mesh of its cage. Cookies)*

TANYA: Here, Boris! That's it. Good girl. Here, Boris.

LEON: What are you feeding the rat?

TANYA: Peanut butter cookies. I was passing the kitchen, and they spoke to me. "Take us along, Tanya!"

LEON: Give me some. I'm starving.

TANYA: Help yourself. You should come to cocktail hour. Free snacks.

LEON: I can't make conversation with those people. Fucking lot lice.

TANYA: They're only people, like you. And me, darling. Even Isaiah Sandoval.

LEON: *(Stuffing cookies in his mouth)* You talked to him?

TANYA: Not enough. I've been trying all week. It's not easy. He's...confused. He's got himself that girl who makes sure he doesn't step off the cliff.

LEON: A wise man. These cliffs are dangerous, especially in the dark. *(Sings)*
The breaking waves dashed high
On the stern and rockbound coast...

TANYA: I hate that song.

LEON: They should have meals at this pigsty.

TANYA: No more pie car, Leon. This is a hotel, such as it is. We can't even pay for the room.

LEON: We'll pay. Once we have Mister Sandoval's little nest egg, we'll pay. What did Eddie say? How much?

TANYA: He only saw it, Leon. He didn't count it.

LEON: What did he say?

TANYA: Two hundred thousand dollars in a child's red plastic suitcase.

LEON: Exactly my recollection, Tanya. His very words.

TANYA: That woman, Helena, isn't as stupid as she looks. Don't overreach, Leon. I don't want you fucking her. I know she's your type.

(LEON *advances toward* TANYA. *His arms are open wide, an unreadable expression on his face.)*

LEON: You are my type. Perfect.

TANYA: Keep your hands off me, Leon, or I'll stab you in your sleep. You won't even know you're dead, Leon.

LEON: You can't live without me, Tanya. You'd starve.

TANYA: I'm starving already.

LEON: Not for long.

(LEON *has finished erecting the puppet theater. He steps behind the booth, sticking his head out into the puppet stage, along with the* DEVIL *glove-puppet on one of his hands. It's a horned, red-faced figure, with a dark cloak, holding a stick.)*

DEVIL: *(A strange squeaky voice)* Are spirits real? Is there life after life? After life?

LEON: Houdini said no. Thurston said yes. After thirty years of psychic exploration, Professor Leon Vole says—I have no fucking idea.

DEVIL: Stupid! Stupid Leon! Stupid little man!!!

(*The* DEVIL *puppet beats* LEON's *face with its stick. Again and again. Blood flows.)*

TANYA: Stop it! Leon, stop it! You'll get blood on the theater.

(*The* DEVIL *is gone, and another puppet rises up to share the stage with* LEON's *head—the* CROCODILE.*)*

CROCODILE: *(Deep voice)* Let me tie you up and love you. Love you and love you and…

*(TANYA laughs in spite of herself. LEON steps out of the booth, the crocodile still on his hand.)*

LEON: Helena will allow us to do a number of public performances here—for the local children.

TANYA: If she gets permission from Mister Whelk, the owner.

LEON: This ballroom is perfect. We'll do The Crystal Castle. Five dollars a head. We need time, and we haven't a sou.

*(A silence)*

LEON: The semifamous Isaiah Sandoval, with his asinine stories.

TANYA: The story's not bad, for a beginning. I'm interested.

*(Outside the hotel, seen through the window at the rear, SCHWARZBERG noisily crosses, drunk and full of memories.)*

SCHWARZBERG: *(Crossing)* Nooze, Nooze or Mirra, Nooze. Nooze.
Getcha Mirra.
Union Square, N train to Dyckman Street, Zerega Avenue, Moshulu Parkway, Sheepshead Bay, Kings Highway… *(He is gone.)*

LEON: I don't deserve this. The Hotel Splendide— drunks and losers.

TANYA: Speaking of losers, Leon, you know our friend Eddie can be a formidable liar…

LEON: Not about this. I could tell.
Did you fuck him?

TANYA: I don't remember.

LEON: Ah, Eddie. Our chauffeur for three weeks. When we had money, after that weekend in Scranton. A lovely young man. The temperament of a rabid spider monkey, and a brain the size of a walnut. Well?

TANYA: I might have. Or maybe I just teased him a bit. Did *you* fuck him?

LEON: Of course. A malleable moron like that— how could I resist? Oh well, what does it matter...

TANYA: Is he dead?

LEON: Why do you assume he died?

TANYA: Don't fool with me, Leon.

LEON: Eddie did have an accident, I believe. Slipped on a motel bathmat, cracked his head open, then staggered off to find medical attention. In his delirium he must have mistaken the dumpster behind Burger King for a medical facility. That's where they will have found him. By now. His wallet had a nude photo of Rose in it. A Polaroid.

(LEON *coughs, and coughs again. He's not well.*)

LEON: Fucking pneumonia.
You know, Tanya, that winter we spent in the Pyrenees broke my health.

(TANYA *goes to the window at the rear. She looks out.*)

(*Sound of the sea*)

TANYA: Black as the grave.

(LEON *laughs, the laughter interrupted by a renewed bout of coughing.*)

## Scene Two

*(The ballroom, later that night)*

*(ROSE stands alone in the ballroom, under the huge chandelier.)*

*(LITTLE JUNIOR appears out of the darkness. He's holding two bottles of beer.)*

LITTLE JUNIOR: You still up?

ROSE: What does it look like?

LITTLE JUNIOR: You could have been sleeping. There's people sleep standing up like that.

ROSE: Not me.

LITTLE JUNIOR: You want a drink? These are cold.

ROSE: O K.

*(LITTLE JUNIOR hands ROSE a beer. They drink.)*

*(She laughs.)*

LITTLE JUNIOR: Why you laughing?

ROSE: I don't know.

LITTLE JUNIOR: You laughing at me?

ROSE: No. No…
I'm just so tired, and I can't sleep.

LITTLE JUNIOR: Me too.
He go to bed?

ROSE: Isaiah?

LITTLE JUNIOR: Yeah. Isaiah.

ROSE: He said he was going to bed, but I don't know. This place is so big, he could be wandering around anywhere.

LITTLE JUNIOR: You look in his room?

ROSE: I can't look in his room. If he's awake and catches me, he gets furious. "What if theres a lady in here? What is the lady gonna think, Rose? What if I'm telling myself a bedtime story, and you interrupt me?" I don't even know if I'm still working for him. Or his family. They don't pay me anymore.

(ROSE *and* LITTLE JUNIOR *drink beer. Long silence*)

ROSE: My ex-boyfriend Eddie was a terrible jerk, you know. Cause of him, I've been a liar and a thief. Now I'm a nurse, sort of.

You know what I know how to do? I can read and write. Adding. Subtracting. Times table. I know how to shoot pool extremely well.

I don't think I know how to make love to someone. Or to earn a living. Or make myself happy. I don't know how to think straight when I need to. I don't know how to pray.

Little Junior, you went to college, didn't you?

LITTLE JUNIOR: Yeah.

ROSE: They teach you any of those things at college?

LITTLE JUNIOR: Well, I...

ROSE: I'm teasing you. I know damn well they don't. Little Junior?

LITTLE JUNIOR: Yeah?

ROSE: I like you.

Tell me something. Where, exactly, do you think we're at? You and me.

LITTLE JUNIOR: A hell of a ways from nowhere, and a long ways to go.

Rose, I'm gonna say goodnight. I'm just standing here, and I don't know what I'm doing anymore. I need to sleep, and I'm wide awake. I'm going walking, down on the rocks.

Look, I…

(LITTLE JUNIOR *goes up to* ROSE *and takes her in his arms. He kisses her.*)

(*After a moment, she pushes him away.*)

LITTLE JUNIOR: You know I'm crazy in love with you. I been in love with you ever since I first saw you.

(LITTLE JUNIOR *tries to kiss* ROSE *again, and she turns away.*)

LITTLE JUNIOR: It doesn't appear to be my tide. Like I say, goodnight, Rose.

(LITTLE JUNIOR *is gone.* ROSE *remains.*)

(*Sound of the sea*)

## Scene Three

(*The ballroom, later that night*)

(*The puppet booth is set up but pushed back toward the wall.* ISAIAH *is on the tattered velvet couch, half dressed.*)

ISAIAH: (*Sings*)
There's a beautiful light on the ocean
Beautiful light on the sea
Beautiful light on the ocean
Where my loved one lies waiting for me…
Molokai, Makinac, Bataan, Island in the Moon.
Ossabaw, Laputa, Treasure Island. Pleasure Island, donkey ears, and…

(HELENA *appears in a bathrobe, with a lantern.*)

ISAIAH: Ah. The landlady. Did I wake you? I'm sorry.

HELENA: You didn't wake me. I was up. I wanted to see you. I talked to Mister Whelk about your situation.

ISAIAH: Situation? Ah! Rose and I—we still seem to be out of funds.

HELENA: Exactly. I'm getting the feeling it's a permanent condition.

ISAIAH: What does Mister Whelk have to say? This can't help finance the villa in Bermuda.

HELENA: Bimini. And it's a two-bedroom condo. Usually Mister Whelk has about as much mercy as God—but he left it to my judgment.

ISAIAH: Judgment?

HELENA: Whether to boot you out on your ass, or let you stay on indefinitely.

(Outside the hotel, seen through the window at the rear, SCHWARZBERG noisily crosses again, back to wherever he came from, drunk and full of memories.)

SCHWARZBERG: Stillwell Avenue, Cropsey Avenue. Nevins! Nevins and DeKalb! Take the local number six all the way. Double L schmancy-Delancey fucking Jerome Avenue up to Gun Hill Road.

HELENA: Mister Schwarzberg! Shut up!

SCHWARZBERG: Getcha Nooze!

HELENA: Go to sleep!

SCHWARZBERG: Nooze or Mirra, Nooze. Getcha Nooze... (He is gone.)

HELENA: Mister S sold newspapers on the New York subway for years. Car to car. Midnight through the morning rush. He hasn't lived in New York for a long time, but his mind still rides the trains.

ISAIAH: I like him.

HELENA: So do I.

ISAIAH: I like it here. Rose hates it.

HELENA: She's young. You in love with her?

ISAIAH: You tell me.

HELENA: I don't think so.
If you can't pay her, she's gonna leave. Eventually.

ISAIAH: She'll go when she's ready.
You want the job?

HELENA: I'm no nursemaid.

ISAIAH: I just get in a little trouble now and then. You
hold my leash and sing me lullabies. It's actually easy
work, extremely high paying...
So. What are you gonna do, Helena? Kick us out?

HELENA: I made my decision.

ISAIAH: And...

HELENA: This is the dark end of the street, Mister
Sandoval. The deep middle of the night time.

ISAIAH: Yes, indeed it is.

HELENA: Beautiful man like you shouldn't have
to worry about a little thing like a hotel bill. *(She
approaches* ISAIAH. *She drops her bathrobe. Underneath
she's wearing silk.)*

HELENA: I'm twenty-eight years old and weigh one
ten in my lingerie. Any man oughta be able to keep his
mind on me—and nobody else.

*(*ISAIAH *takes her in his arms. They spin slowly under the
flickering chandelier.)*

## Scene Four

*(A huge noise, as if two people have fallen into a pile
of garbage cans right outside, interrupts this romantic
moment.)*

*(*SCHWARZBERG *and* LITTLE JUNIOR *enter, drunk, sloppy,
and singing. They are barefoot, shoes hanging around their
necks.)*

*(The magic moment under the chandelier is over.)*

LITTLE JUNIOR & SCHWARZBERG: *(Sloppy, off-key doo-wop)*
Doo doo doo, here in my heart
Theres a story untold
Of a girl who left me standing, standing in the cold
And since she went awayyyyy
I've never had a happy dayyy...

LITTLE JUNIOR: *(Noticing* HELENA *and* ISAIAH*)* Oooh
wee. We pissed in the churchyard now.

*(*HELENA *is thoroughly annoyed, puts on her robe.* ISAIAH *is amused.)*

HELENA: What the hell do you two mean by...

SCHWARZBERG: We are moonlight drunks. I'm teaching
Little Junior, Chinese style, so we can recite poems to
each other. Li Po, Tu Fu, and the boys, out in a rowboat
with a jug of California Chablis. Row row row your
boat, gently down the...down the...

LITTLE JUNIOR: I took him way out onto the rocks, by
the deepest tide pools.

SCHWARZBERG: I even looked in, and you know I don't
like mirrors. He tells me this one pool gives visions.
Pictures in the black water. We do great things under
the moon.
You know, Isaiah, you should come out there with us
instead of talking to the chandelier.

ISAIAH: Are you drunk too, Little Junior?

LITTLE JUNIOR: Me? I'm not drunk. I've been making
sure Mister S doesn't fall off the cliff.

SCHWARZBERG: I'm trying to look God right in the eye.

HELENA: Mister S, get out of here. Both of you, go to
sleep.

SCHWARZBERG: Can't. Education. I gotta educate Little Junior here. Nowadays, everything is cool, moderne, streamline, so I'm teaching him to be a streamline man.

ISAIAH: Take me back out there. We'll dive through the sea foam to where the mermaids swim. Coral bones. Hammerheads. Strange creatures down below.

LITTLE JUNIOR: No stranger than us.

SCHWARZBERG: You see. Streamline philosophy.

(SCHWARZBERG *falls onto the sofa.* HELENA *wraps her robe around her, lights a cigarette.*)

(LITTLE JUNIOR *carefully empties his pockets of small sea creatures, shells, and driftglass. He lays his treasures out around him…*)

SCHWARZBERG: I remember before I was born, the bells ringing. I was a boy in the city by the river. I had a toy boat.

Vilnius. Far away.

I still can see the faces, the dirty black robes. The smell of dead chickens and piss.

*(He sings a lilting, mournful song.)*
Di di di di di di di di, ay ay di di di
Di di di, Dee ay di di
Dee ay di di dee di
Ahhh aaaaaah
Di di di di di…

There is a goddess of overpowering sadness, and she rules my life. She drowns me. I'm dying.

LITTLE JUNIOR: Forget all that shit about the old country, Mister S.

SCHWARZBERG: You have ears, Little Junior? I'm dying. I've gotta GO. So I'm remembering, my tongue to your ear. I'm saving my life in *your* head. So when I die, all that shit will be saved. Vilnius, my toy boat—all of it. That's what the world is made of, Little Junior. All that

shit. *(Sings again, livelier)*
Di di di di di di di di, ay ay ay ayyyy, di di di di di...

*(ISAIAH gets up, heads toward the door.)*

HELENA: Isaiah? Where you going?

ISAIAH: I'm not sure. Maybe out on the cliffs.

HELENA: Not alone, you don't. Those rocks are slick,
and, moon or no moon, it's dark out there.

*(ISAIAH, on his way out of the ballroom, pauses.)*

ISAIAH: Helena, we'll finish our dance sometime...

HELENA: Sure. Sure we will.

*(ISAIAH exits.)*

SCHWARZBERG: You see, Helena. Little Junior is a drunk
genius. A boy wonder.

HELENA: You and Boy Wonder interrupted a romantic
moment I had going there.

SCHWARZBERG: Bigger and bigger tide pools he's
gonna find. You know he's got a saltwater tank for sea
animals out behind the garden?
I'm teaching him—about life and death.

LITTLE JUNIOR: And slivovitz.

HELENA: Assholes.


## Scene Five

*(The ballroom, much later that night)*

*(ISAIAH wanders like a ghost, his pants wet up to the knee.)*

*(ROSE appears. She's pulled on a pair of jeans and a shirt.
She's barefoot.)*

ROSE: If you can't sleep, at least sit still, dammit. These
boards creak, and I don't know about everyone else
in this hotel, but I been thinking a wolf is crawling

through the hallways, or some creature from the sea is slithering up here looking for his human bride.

ISAIAH: Sorry I woke you.

ROSE: Sure you are. Sit down, before Mister Schwarzberg comes out with a pistol and shoots you for a prowler.

ISAIAH: The night time is the right time.

ROSE: Give me a break, O K? No talk about suicide at four a.m. *(Noticing his wet pants)* Where you been?

ISAIAH: Fishing. In the tide pools.

ROSE: Oh, Jesus.

*(ISAIAH sits, holding his head in his hands. He may be weeping, but we can't tell. ROSE begins to sing, hesitantly at first, then with too much good cheer.)*

ROSE: *(Sings)*
Zip-a-dee doo-dah, zip-a-dee ay
My oh my what a wonderful day
Plenty of sunshine, heading my way
Zip-a-dee doo-dah…

ISAIAH: Not that. Please. Not Mister Bluebird.

ROSE: I'm trying here, Isaiah.

ISAIAH: Sing me something else. Sing me the song I taught you.

ROSE: You'll go to bed?

ISAIAH: O K, Rose. I'll try.

*(ROSE sings, very solemnly and beautifully.)*

ROSE: *(Sings)*
Farewell and adieu, to you Spanish ladies
Farewell and adieu, to you ladies of Spain
Our captains commanded we sail for New England
So we may never see you again.
Farewell and adieu, to you Spanish ladies

Farewell and adieu, to you ladies of Spain
We sail tonight, for the New Bedford light
So we may never see you again.

ISAIAH: Thank you, Rose. I'd do the same for you, but I can't sing.

ROSE: Fuck you.
*(A long silence)*
Isaiah—what were their names?

ISAIAH: They don't have names anymore.

ROSE: They have names. Your wife, and your children, they have names.

ISAIAH: They're dead, you know. I was driving, we crashed, and they died. All my pretty ones. All three. I walked away without a scratch, Rose.

ROSE: I know the story, Isaiah. I just want you to…

ISAIAH: Rose, maybe you should just shut up, cause you have no idea what you are talking about.

ROSE: Excuse me? I'm the girl who's been pulling you from in front of trains, giving you medicine that makes you stupid, apologizing for how rude you are to every big-eyed lit major who wants an autograph. I been right next to you for two years.

ISAIAH: I'm sorry, Rose. I'm not gonna start a shiny new life.
Man is born to sorrow as the sparks fly upward. Well, they're flying, ain't they.

ROSE: I'm trying to get you talking. That's all.

ISAIAH: You become some kind of therapist, Rose?

ROSE: I'm just another person, Isaiah. They died three years ago. Three years is a long time.

ISAIAH: Not to me.

ROSE: You don't think straight sometimes, you know.
Even when you think you do. If it was someone else
it wouldn't matter so much, but it's you, and it's a
terrible waste.
Besides, I get scared you won't come back.

ISAIAH: I'm not scared of that. Don't you be, Rose.
This world is a Saturday matinee horror movie. We're
just zooming through the darkness, screaming our
lungs out, with our fucking heads on fire. No one's
listening.

ROSE: I'm listening.
I listen to you all the time.
*(Silence)*
You got to the ocean, as far away as you could get. We
made a good run. The ocean here is gray and rough.
It's good for you.
You could be writing stuff again, you know. You're
writing that story. The one about Coconut Joe.

ISAIAH: Not writing. That's a true story. A whisper in
my ear.

*(Silence)*

ROSE: You want your medicine?

ISAIAH: I want a bottle of champagne.

ROSE: See. You won't take your medicine.

ISAIAH: No more pills, Rosie. I mean it this time. I'll live
or die without them.
So say goodnight, Rose.

*(ROSE doesn't move.)*

ISAIAH: Not yet? So, bedtime story. To thank you for
your kindness.
In the Coconut Mountains. No. It's Coconut Joe in the
mountains, and the air is bitter cold, and he weeps. His
skin bubbles with pus, and his brain is burning.

The story of Coconut Joe, part two.

*(Crossfade: The Story of Coconut Joe, Part Two)*

*(Snow everywhere.* COCONUT JOE *and the* RAGGEDY MAN *stand in line. The figure in a full-body* ANTIRADIATION SUIT *addresses them.)*

ANIT-RADIATION SUIT: DIRTBAGS! The motto of the Italo-Germanic Nuclear Waste Disposal Corporation is? IS?

COCONUT JOE & RAGGEDY MAN: "Nowhere To Go."

ANIT-RADIATION SUIT: So true. Climb up, and die on the impassable ice-covered peak. Climb down, and we shoot you in the head.
This meeting is over. Please resume your duties.

*(*COCONUT JOE *and the* RAGGEDY MAN *shovel.)*

ISAIAH: Coconut Joe and his new-found friend are up to their waists in glowing sludge, which they shovel onto an endless conveyor belt. They itch horribly, and their skin is turning green.

RAGGEDY MAN: I started out with the Ackerman-Zorbaugh Shows, playing little dink towns. I was on the looper. Second man.

COCONUT JOE: You're an American? Like me.

RAGGEDY MAN: Fuckin' A.

COCONUT JOE: What are you doing here? I mean, how did you…

RAGGEDY MAN: Last job, I was with the Vivona Brothers on Royal American. We had ten diesel light plants. Whole midway lit up like a Christmas tree. This place surprise you?

COCONUT JOE: Well, I never…

RAGGEDY MAN: It doesn't surprise me. I been around the world with shows three times. Australia, Japan,

Mongolia, Venezuela, up with the Eskimos. Wherever you go, people are crazy, cruel, and heartless. Being a sonofabitch is a universal human trait.

COCONUT JOE: Not everyone is...

RAGGEDY MAN: Every man, or woman, is willing to cause intolerable pain to his neighbor for a moment's personal pleasure. Or a dollar. Or a deutsche mark. Or a yen. Or a...

ANIT-RADIATION SUIT: Get to work, you!

(COCONUT JOE *and* RAGGEDY MAN *work.*)

COCONUT JOE: Is there a pass over that mountain?

RAGGEDY MAN: You're kidding, my friend. That's the Devil's Hatband. It's never been climbed. Most of Hannibal's elephants died up there, before he turned back and went to Italy by sea.

COCONUT JOE: Hannibal? Who's...

RAGGEDY MAN: Hannibal of Carthage. I'm a professor of European history.

COCONUT JOE: Professor, I just realized, just by being here, my chromosomes are probably screwed up for life. If I ever have another child, she'll be a mutant.

RAGGEDY MAN: You don't have to worry about your mutant children, my friend.

COCONUT JOE: Why not?

RAGGEDY MAN: They'll never exist.
You'll die here, in this pit of bone-eating sewage.

COCONUT JOE: I'll die here—and so will you.

RAGGEDY MAN: *(Laughs)* Not me. I've been exposing myself to increasing degrees of radiation in a controlled, scientific manner. I'm a professor of molecular biology, you know. Yesterday I carried a fuel rod to the pit with my bare hands. The guards couldn't believe it. Assholes.

I've become immune. In fact, I feel stronger than ever. My mind is working double shifts. The radiation has cleaned my brain of all the muck and twisted thoughts that made me do all those terrible...

*(A grimace of sudden pain crosses the* RAGGEDY MAN's *face. He clutches his chest, surprised.)*

RAGGEDY MAN: No wonder. *(He drops down dead at* COCONUT JOE's *feet.)*

COCONUT JOE: Holy shit. This is worse than I thought. Everyone is dying from radiation sickness, and the only way out is over the—Devil's Hatband.

*(The* RAGGEDY MAN *rises from death, to say these last words.)*

RAGGEDY MAN: Nowhere to gooooooooo!

*(The* RAGGEDY MAN *dies again.* COCONUT JOE *looks up toward the peak.)*

ISAIAH: Coconut Joe from Kokomo, dressed in rags, radiation blisters on his body, crawls up toward the peak of the Devil's Hatband. Shards of ice tear at his freezing body. He wants to end the pain, to throw himself over the edge—yet he goes on. His daughter back in Kokomo needs him! Universal Bake Shoppe needs the coconut! It begins to snow again, more heavily than ever, in large soft flakes...

*(Hush of snow, mountain wind. Joe crawls desperately upward. A beautiful female hallucination,* THE SNOW SPIRIT, *appears.)*

THE SNOW SPIRIT: *(Sings)* Ahhhhhh, ahhhhh, ahhhhhhhhh. Ooooooohh ooooooh hoooo JOE! JOE ISKOWITZ! I love you. Come to me! I need you...

COCONUT JOE: No! No!

THE SNOW SPIRIT: Stay here with me, in the swirling snow. Lie down and rest, on this soft whiteness. Lie down and rest. *(Sings)* Ahhhh ahhhhhh ahhhhhhh... *(Continuing under)*

COCONUT JOE: No! No...

ISAIAH: The world was white, and the snow smelled like coconut, flakes of Zamboanga pure floating around him like tiny fairies.
Somehow, he keeps on.
At last, he crawls to the summit and rolls, rolls down the other side of the mountain—into ITALY!

*(Music. Italian, of course)*

ISAIAH: Still high in the mountains, Coconut Joe looks across a field of snow and sees something—something he can't believe. A huge blue star in the snow. Steam rises from the blue star. A swimming pool?

*(From a distance, laughter and chatter of naked people, in many languages, continuing under...)*

ISAIAH: And around it there are people, beautiful naked men and beautiful naked women, swimming naked in a star-shaped pool in the middle of the snow. With a waiter in black tie bringing them drinks. Coconut Joe is hallucinating.

COCONUT JOE: I'm hallucinating!

ISAIAH: He faints into a snowbank.

WOMAN AT THE POOL: Marcello! *Posso trovare l'uomo qui a fainto?*

WAITER: *Si, signorina.*

ISAIAH: Joe wakes inside a very curious mountain spa.

*(All the SPA GUESTS are very international, attractive, in their twenties. They've put fashionable spa outfits on.)*

SPA GUEST 1: *Buon giorno.* Hello there. Welcome to Strella Novo, our institute for personal rejuvenation.

SPA GUEST 2: Are you the pool boy?

COCONUT JOE: I'm an American. Joe Iskowitz. You folks heard of Universal Bake Shoppe? The Coconut Dee-Lite Cookie?

*(Silence)*

SPA GUEST 3: We are a cult of wealthy industrialists.

SPA GUEST 1: Film stars.

SPA GUEST 2: And fashion designers.

SPA GUEST 3: We believe in the invigorating powers of a certain drug made from the lemur, an Indonesian monkey.

SPA GUEST 4: The medicine keeps us young. Very young.

SPA GUEST 1: I'm seventy-eight years old.

SPA GUEST 2: I'm a hundred and seven.

SPA GUEST 3: I'm a hundred forty-eight years old. Feel my belly. My arms. My ass.

COCONUT JOE: Look, folks, that's great, but I need to find out about my coconut shipment and get home to my daughter.

SPA GUEST 1: I'm so, how you say, unhappy to tell you. The only way out of Strella Novo is by air. The next plane isn't due for six months.

SPA GUEST 2: Relax. Ease your mind, Mister Coconut Joe. You're among friends.

SPA GUEST 3: Put him to work in the lemur lab.

SPA GUEST 1: It's an honor, Joe. It's where we take the lives of the monkeys, to make the drug that keeps us forever young.

*(They put a lab coat on* COCONUT JOE.*)*

*(Science music)*

ISAIAH: Strella Novo—a world of love and pleasure, where nobody ages and nothing ever changes.

SPA GUEST 1: Joe, when things stop happening, they happen fast.

*(The* SPA GUESTS *are gone.)*

ISAIAH: Joe assists a certain Doctor Moto from Japan, a silent, efficient technician.

*(The spa lab.* COCONUT JOE *and* DR MOTO *work in tandem, making serum out of dead monkeys.* COCONUT JOE *passes him the monkeys, and* MOTO *extracts something. They chuck the used corpses in a huge pile.)*

MOTO: Next! Ah… Next! Ah… Next! Ah… Next! Ah…

COCONUT JOE: Doc, will these monkeys last forever? I mean, is the supply unlimited? You know, plenty monkey?

MOTO: Plenty monkey? Yankee idiot. These are the last lemurs anywhere. The bribe paid to the government of Indonesia to get these out was ten million dollars. And a million to Save the Animals, to ignore the lemur question.

COCONUT JOE: What happens when these are gone?

MOTO: The lemur serum addicts will age rather rapidly, I imagine. *(Laughs)* Ten years in ten minutes. I'll be blamed for the unfortunate turn of events, and some of the rapidly wrinkling populace may be armed. I'm leaving Strella Novo. Tonight.

COCONUT JOE: It's impossible.

MOTO: Giulietta Mascarpone, the Italian film star and her bodyguard leave at midnight by private helicopter.

I knock out the bodyguard with a few drops of somnambutal, dress in his clothes, and…

COCONUT JOE: Where are they going?

MOTO: Venice, city of sewage.

COCONUT JOE: Venice? That's where my coconut shipment is loading.
Listen, Doctor Moto. I've got an idea.

MOTO: Are you surprised I speak your language? I was educated at Oxford, then Yale and…

COCONUT JOE: Shut up, and listen!

*(Darkness and the whirring of helicopter blades. Lights of a helicopter landing. In those lights, MOTO in an expensive bodyguard suit, with a headset and a pistol. COCONUT JOE wears sunglasses and a low-cut sheath dress.)*

COCONUT JOE: *(Italian movie starlet voice) Ciao, bambini!* Venezia, and step on it!

*(In a whirl of light, they're gone. The beautiful people of Strella Novo look up after the helicopter. They grow older, and older.)*

ISAIAH: By the way, before he left Strella Novo, Coconut Joe let all the remaining lemur monkeys out of their cages. They escaped into the snow, where they all died, of course, being tropical creatures.

*(The SPA GUESTS wander aimlessly, drooling and senile.)*

SPA GUESTS: Leeemurrr… Leeemurrrrrr… Leeemurrrr…

*(They're gone.)*

GONDOLIER 1: *(Sings) O sole mio… (Continuing…)*

*(Still in his sheath dress, COCONUT JOE arrives in Venice.)*

GONDOLIER 2: Welcome to Venice! Eh, you! Get off the boat!

ISAIAH: Once in Venice, Joe discovers there's a telephone strike and a postal strike.

COCONUT JOE: Shit. My daughter must be pretty worried by now. And Mister Krumm and Universal Bake Shoppe must be going nuts.

Well, the coconut's almost all loaded in the harbor. Guess I'll check into this place on the canal—the Sfogliatelli Hotel and Gardens. Looks like a dump, but what the hey. It's only for a few days.

DESK CLERK: Aren't you Giulietta Mascar...

COCONUT JOE: Shut up.

ISAIAH: Coconut Joe sits in his room. In the hallway, a chambermaid is singing a song from her own country, far away...

ROSE: *(Singing a song in a strange language)*
Bala la la, kala la la
Ohshka lama lai de dai
Bala la la Kala la la
Ya dorai shami, bambi saidi
Ohshka lama lai de dai...

ISAIAH: Up above the immortal city of Venice, the night is intensely blue. The stars pulse in the sky like white sea creatures. Down below, the streetlamp in front of the Sfogliatelli Hotel sheds a filmy sphere of yellow light, streaked by the blue-green of its neon sign.

The earth is still, between breaths.

*(Crossfade back to Hotel Splendide ballroom)*

## Scene Six

*(The ballroom. Edge of dawn)*

*(On the velvet couch is* TANYA *Near her is* ISAIAH.*)*

*(In another area, the puppet theater is set up in the shadows. Its curtain opens slowly to reveal the face of* LEON. *He watches in silence.)*

ISAIAH: City of mist and mellow…mellow stones. City of drowning…drowning in the frightening beauty of a schoolgirl, a flight of… No. The sulphurous gloom, the lantern, the black water of the canal…

TANYA: Can you do my dreaming for me sometime?

ISAIAH: No one can do that.

TANYA: Go on. I'm listening.

ISAIAH: No. There was nothing there. Waste of time.

TANYA: Liar.

*(*ISAIAH *laughs. He moves closer to* TANYA. *Light brightens on* LEON *within the puppet theater.)*

LEON: Behold the shepherd Acis, about to kiss the sandals, the thighs, the lips of the nymph Galatea— while the menacing fife of one-eyed Polyphemus already sounds close at hand—if he could only hear it!

ISAIAH: The night is almost over.
Dance for me.

TANYA: *(Laughs)* I used to dance for everyone. On the Spanish web, high above the crowd. I've come down to earth.

ISAIAH: Then tell me a story.

TANYA: I thought that was your thing—telling stories to help fools pass the time.

ISAIAH: You're a hard mistress for a sick man.

TANYA: Because I've lived.

And you're not sick. You're drowning in your own unhappiness.

I won't tell you a story, but I'll tell you something true. At times our puppet theater performs in the cancer wards of children's hospitals. All the beds are drawn close together so the patients connected to feeding tubes, or on the morphine drip, can see the show. The beds have snowy white sheets and pillows. They wear white hospital gowns. In this whiteness are the faces and eager eyes of the dying children. Like droplets of fire.

They laugh at our show—all of them. Even the ones in pain.

I'll tell you something else. I'm in love.

ISAIAH: Beautiful woman like you, your husband's a lucky man.

TANYA: Leon's not lucky. He's terribly unfortunate.

And I don't love him anymore.

I love you.

ISAIAH: Sure. That's the way it ought to be. Everybody love everybody else. Be a better world. Be a…

TANYA: Isaiah, shhh. Pay attention, please.

I want you. This is not a joke, or a silly flirtation. Let's go to your room. You have a room, don't you?

ISAIAH: This is a hotel.

Everybody has a room.

*(Light intensifies on* LEON *within the puppet theater.)*

*(*TANYA *moves toward* ISAIAH.*)*

*(*ISAIAH *moves toward* TANYA *and takes her in his arms.)*

*(The chandelier flickers and goes out.)*

LEON: And around the puppet theater our carnival turns, and around the turning carnival, our turning world.

*(The puppet theater curtain closes.)*

## END ACT ONE

# ACT TWO

*(The Hotel Splendide on a peninsula, its bare, ruined public rooms, and its garden. Two weeks later.)*

## PART ONE
### In The Hotel—Day
### Scene One

*(The ballroom, midday)*

*(Overcast, gray light. The chandelier is off. The same odd collection of furniture. The rat wheel is still set up, toward the rear. LEON is working on the puppet theater, in preparation for a show. TANYA watches him.)*

*(There's a tray of drinks and snacks. LITTLE JUNIOR's got his waiters jacket on, and he brings a tall one to TANYA.)*

*(He looks in the rat's cage.)*

LITTLE JUNIOR: Boris looks like you haven't fed him in a couple days.

TANYA: In hard times, even the rats suffer.

LITTLE JUNIOR: That's crap. You could have found him something.
Here, Boris.

*(LITTLE JUNIOR feeds the rat off his snack tray—pretzels.)*

TANYA: You should have a talk with my husband. He's a self-righteous bastard, just like you. In his way. Go ahead.

LITTLE JUNIOR: He looks busy.

TANYA: Preparing for our show today. You'll see it, of course.

(ISAIAH *enters, wanders over to the puppet theater.*)

LEON: Leave that alone, Mister Sandoval. It's easily set askew.

(ISAIAH *plays with the curtain, the decor.*)

ISAIAH: Pitch your tent below the waves. Near Mindanao. Voodoo starfish.

LEON: What the fuck are you doing?

(ISAIAH *wanders away from the theater.*)

ISAIAH: Ava and her shock-o-rama pajama party girls!

LEON: Don't touch my things again. Not ever.

ISAIAH: Sorry. I'm sorry, I was just…

(ISAIAH *wanders off to a chair, sprawls, his mind wandering.*)

ISAIAH: …I was just there, and she was just there—like the people on the news who get hit by the train. Hell of an accident. Sunset Limited. There it goes. Pulls up at the Sonic Drive-In. A to Z Cash Pawn. Plutonium Road. I loved her, but that didn't seem to help matters. Not in the end.?
Zam-bo-an-ga. Zamboanga. Where's my buddy? He's lost…

(LITTLE JUNIOR *approaches* LEON.)

LITTLE JUNIOR: Mister Vole, could I try to work the puppets?

LEON: No.

Not a boy who loves nothing but the wiggle of the
fiddler crab and the luminescence of the sea. Not a
boy who loves nothing but the zip-zing of Hungarian
bands and the erotical hum of the neon. Understand
me, please. This is a noble trade.

(ROSE *comes in, looking for* ISAIAH. *She spots him, and she's
furious.*)

ROSE: Isaiah, I been looking for you. Running all
around this place. I even went out on the rocks. I
thought you'd fallen into the sea.

ISAIAH: Right down to the bottom. Full fathom five.

ROSE: Bullshit. I don't want you going wherever the
hell you were all by yourself.

ISAIAH: I was right here, in this pleasant company. All
morning.

ROSE: I don't give a fuck where you've been. Just don't
lie to me, O K? I don't deserve it.
Little Junior, can I get a drink, please.

LITTLE JUNIOR: Sure. You want a club soda?

ROSE: I want a rum and Coke.
Hey, the puppet theatre looks good.

TANYA: Thank you.

ROSE: I need a new occupation. You think I could learn
to work the puppets?

LEON: Let us enter together the Hall of Harmonious
Interest.

TANYA: I don't advise it. It's no longer a lively sector of
show business. And the art takes years to attain. You
need to start young.
Leon's father, Ivan Vasilievitch Vole, was a puppeteer,
a maestro. He started Leon passing the hat when he
was five years old.

Ivan Vasilievitch suffered from alcoholism, a Russian talent. The last time we went to his house in Saint Petersburg—we hadn't seen him for five years—it was by sled, over the dazzling snow of March. A young woman heard the bells and thrust her head out of a casement window. "You want to see Ivan? You missed him. He's dead. He was buried last Monday. If you're his son Leon, he told me to give you these."
She threw them out the window, the bitch. They landed in the snow. Two ragged handpuppets—the Devil, and the Devil's Crocodile.
Quite the dying gift.
Old bastard.
The puppets feed us, give us drink, clothe us. We live through them, but so do they, through us.

(HELENA *enters. She goes up to* LEON *and* TANYA.)

HELENA: Mister Whelk said no. No public performances in the hotel.

LEON: Fucking philistine.

TANYA: Our posters are up in town. The theater is ready. Leon has prepared his…

HELENA: No.

LEON: Why?

HELENA: I have no idea. Maybe Mister Whelk hates little puppets.
You might try the library in town. Or there's a parking lot…

TANYA: Miss Skate, please. You must understand. The Vole Family Theater is not a…

LEON: If the theatricals can't be public, perhaps a private showing. If you're pleased by what you see, perhaps your next talk with Mister Whelk might be more persuasive.

HELENA: Do the show if you like…but I doubt Mister Whelk's mind will change.

LEON: We'll see, won't we?

Now, please, SILENCE. And the precious gift of your attention.

(LEON *disappears into the puppet booth. As* TANYA *takes her position near the stage, the devil puppet appears in front of the curtain. He's a red glove puppet with a devil's face and horns. He has grown enormously fat. He has a large donut. He lays it onstage. He bends over, farts at the audience. He eats his donut voraciously.*)

TANYA: Ah. There he is. Our Master of Ceremonies— Uncle Nuncle. How are you, Uncle?

NUNCLE: *(Eating)* Mmmph mmmurppph…

TANYA: Please, Uncle Nuncle. Say hello to everyone here at the Hotel Splendide.

NUNCLE: Hotel Splendide? What a dump! Urp. Fuck it. *(Keeps eating donut)*

TANYA: Uncle Nuncle, you've gotten awfully fat lately.

NUNCLE: From eating children. And donuts.

(NUNCLE *pauses for a moment. The* CROCODILE *sneaks up onstage, grabs the donut in its teeth.*)

NUNCLE: No! Gimme that glazed!

(NUNCLE, *in a wild fury, beats the* CROCODILE *without mercy.*)

NUNCLE: Take that! And that! And that!

(*Finally the* CROCODILE *lets go of the donut and disappears beneath the stage.* NUNCLE *calls after him.*)

NUNCLE: Fuck you.

TANYA: Please, Nuncle. Not so much vulgar language. There are children in the audience.

NUNCLE: Where? Little fuckers. (*Peers out*) Ah, there
they are. Brats. Wheeze wheeze wheeze. My fucking
asthma! Shit. One of you has a pocket full of cat hair!
Dandelions! Wheeze. Nurse Tanya, give me my
medicine!

(TANYA *finds an asthma puffer, hands it to* NUNCLE. *He
takes a huge puff, holds his breath, then hurls the puffer
offstage.*)

NUNCLE: Yeah. High as a kite on this shit. Now. Where
were we, Tanya honey?

TANYA: We're going to put on a show for our friends.

NUNCLE: Intermission! Soda and cookie on the table!
Coconut Dee-Lite!

TANYA: Now, in the dark, magic!

(*The lights dim onstage, except on* TANYA *and the brightly
lit puppet booth.*)

TANYA: Our play: *The Crystal Castle!*

NUNCLE: Boring! Fuck! Insipid. The worst!

TANYA: Ah, I know.
Our play: *The Hermit and the Bear!*

NUNCLE: Fuckin' classic. I love it. The best.

(*To the sound of munching donut,* NUNCLE *disappears.*
TANYA *moves off to one side.*)

TANYA: *The Hermit And The Bear!*

(*Music of the puppet theater, and the curtain opens. A forest
scene, and a simple hut, in cutaway. The* HERMIT *appears, a
bearded figure in a gray robe, carrying a loaf of bread.*)

TANYA: A holy hermit walks through the woods
toward his hut.

HERMIT: (*Chanting*) Amo, amas, amat, amamus…

TANYA: Suddenly, a ferocious bear appears.

*(The* BEAR *rears up to attack.)*

BEAR: GRRRR!

TANYA: The hermit, realizing the bear is hungry, gives him his loaf of bread.

*(The* BEAR *eats.)*

TANYA: The Bear is thankful. He rubs up against the hermit like a pet dog.

BEAR: *(Purring)* Mmmmmm. Mmmm.

*(The* HERMIT *and the* BEAR *embrace. They go to the hut, where the* HERMIT *takes out a hairbrush.)*

TANYA: Back at the hut, the hermit brushes the bear's fur. They eat dinner and go to sleep, a happy pair.

HERMIT: *(Drifting off to sleep)* Amo, amas, amat...

TANYA: The next day, they cut wood together in the forest.

*(The* HERMIT *and the* BEAR *take out a two-man saw and cut a log together.)*

TANYA: They carry the wood back to the hut. The hermit is tired. He takes a nap.

*(The* HERMIT *lies down, and sleeps.)*

TANYA: The bear watches over him, so that nothing will disturb the sleep of his holy friend.

*(A fly buzzes. The* HERMIT *stirs in his sleep.)*

*(The* BEAR *swats at the fly with a heavy paw. Buzzz. Swat. Silence. Buzzz. The hermit almost wakes, stirring in his sleep, head twitching. Swat. Silence. Is it dead? BUZZ.)*

BEAR: Grrrr! *(He picks up a big boulder. He looks for the fly.)*

TANYA: The bear picks up a large boulder. Intent on helping his friend, he...

*(Buzzzzzz. The fly is on the* HERMIT's *nose. His head twitches. The* BEAR *brings the boulder down mightily on the fly. The buzzing stops.)*

TANYA: The fly is dead. And the hermit's head is crushed.

*(The* HERMIT's *head rolls off his body and off the puppet stage, trailing a skein of silk, red as blood. The* BEAR, *trapped in the theatre, cannot reach it.* TANYA *brings the head of his dead friend to the* BEAR.)

TANYA: The bear cradles the holy hermit's head in his paws.

*(The* BEAR *weeps and weeps...)*

*(*TANYA *steps in front of the stage.)*

TANYA: The continuing creation of the world depends on the tears of our Bear. The sun spins around this puppet booth. Everyone beholds us—those who did not come, and those who are not yet born, and those who are long dead—even so, we know that all can see.

*(The curtain falls. The show is over.)*

TANYA: You like it?
My little church for the kiddies.

*(Applause from everyone.* LEON *emerges from behind the puppet booth. The* CROCODILE *puppet is on one of his hands. In the other is a tin cup.)*

LEON: A little something for the showman. Whatever you can spare.

*(*HELENA, LITTLE JUNIOR, ROSE, SCHWARZBERG *all find coins or bills to drop in.)*

*(*ISAIAH *pats his pockets. He reaches into one. He finds nothing.)*

ISAIAH: I don't have anything to give you.

LEON: You're lying, Mister Sandoval. The showman knows.

(ISAIAH *reaches into another pocket. He finds a starfish.*)

ISAIAH: A starfish.

(*He holds it out to* LEON. *The* CROCODILE *on* LEON's *hand makes a frightening sound.*)

LEON: That isn't amusing. Do you want to insult my...

ISAIAH: I wasn't being...

LITTLE JUNIOR: Isaiah, you're being an asshole.

(LITTLE JUNIOR *drops coins in the cup for* ISAIAH.)

LITTLE JUNIOR: Now give me back the starfish before it dies. You took it out of my tank, didn't you?

ROSE: Lay off him, O K. He goofs sometimes, that's all.

LITTLE JUNIOR: That's not a toy for writers. It's an animal, and it lives in the sea. Give it to me. I'll put it back.

ISAIAH: Give it to him, Rose.

(ROSE *takes the starfish, gives it to* LITTLE JUNIOR. *He takes it and exits.*)

## Scene Two

(*The Ballroom, later in the day*)

(ROSE, TANYA, HELENA)

(HELENA *is dancing with herself and singing.*)

HELENA: (*Sings, slow and bluesy*)
Come here, Mister Moonlight
Sit down on your Mama's knee
I want to tell you, baby
How you're sending me
Well, if that's your secret

You better keep it to yourself
Cause if you tell me
I might tell somebody else
Now you can take me, Mister Moonlight
Jump me in your Hollywood bed
And eagle rock me, baby
`Til my face turns cherry red...turns cherry red...
That's all I remember.

ROSE: I met Eddie in a pool hall. Two days later he
moved into my place. Week after that he ran across
some paper and some I D and we started busting
checks. It all went on cars and apartments and getting
high. I had one check left. I knew it was hot but I took a
chance. I needed two hundred for this dress.
They gave me a year with the good girls. I learned
raising flowers in a big greenhouse. Five months,
and I never heard a word from him. One day I'm on
work release, me and thirty other girls picking trash
off the shoulder on the rural route and this fucked-up
Plymouth Duster pulls over near me. "I love you," he
says. "Get in the car." We move into this Motel 6. Not
my dream date. Eddie keeps going out, saying shit
like, "Just sit tight till I get back. Watch T V." He comes
back, he wants to drink two beers, then slap me around
or fuck me.
I wanted to kill him, but I didn't have the nerve. Then
I met Isaiah in a supermarket checkout line. He didn't
even know me and he offered me a job right there in
the Pick and Pay. He'd been sent by whatever power
watches over stupid young women.
We go back to the motel to get my things. Eddie was
there. He objected to my new employment. Isaiah pulls
out a pistol and sticks it in Eddie's ear. He told him
he'd blow his brains out if he ever came looking for
me.

HELENA: Isaiah did that?

ROSE: Yeah.

*(Long silence. She sings quietly, an old country song.)*
Little girl, little girl, don't lie to me
Tell me, where did you sleep last night?
In the pines, in the pines
Where the sun never shines
We'll shiver the whole night through

The longest train I ever saw
Went down that Georgia line
In the pines, in the pines
Where the sun never shines
We'll shiver the whole night through

Little girl, little girl, where'd you sleep last night?
Not even your mother knows
In the pines, in the pines
Where the sun never shines
We'll shiver when the cold wind blows...

HELENA: Once upon a time I knew a great number
of men, every one of whom was, basically, a selfish
moron. Just lately, however, here at the Hotel
Splendide, I been doing well. With men. Mister
Schwarzberg is a gentleman and an artiste, though
a few years too old for me. I hired Little Junior. He's
young, simple-hearted, and only moderately fucked
up. He showed me the tide pools in the rocks and
the cheapest place in town to buy margarita mix. He
was actually kind to me. Its a pity he's a few years too
young, plus I require a certain amount of style.
Now, Isaiah Sandoval—I'll take him anytime, problems
and all.

ROSE: He's a lot of trouble.

HELENA: You don't know what trouble is, honey.
Believe me, you don't.

*(TANYA sings a slow mournful song in a strange language.)*

TANYA: *(Sings)* Laia ladaia
Verouk vashti li skopane
Laia ladiaia ave amah no carita
Cielos avodah vola ciela vola
Laiaia ladaia ma moumiya
Latcho li skopane laia ladaia
Laia ladaia...
You know what I believe?
People pray too damn much. What are they praying
for? Money? Love? Heaven? They're going to get there
anyway. There's no other hell but this one down here.

## Scene Three

*(The ballroom, midafternoon)*

*(SCHWARZBERG is on a ladder, trying to repair the flickering chandelier. He's got pliers, rolls of wire, electrical tape.)*

*(TANYA is on the sofa.)*

SCHWARZBERG: Once I was riding in a boxcar in the winter. I broke up a wooden pallet and started a fire to keep warm. Doing fine, until the fire burns a hole in the car floor. The wind blows up through that little hole, sparks flying. The whole car catches fire, walls burning everywhere. I jumped off into the snow, landed in a drift alongside the track. Off goes the boxcar, a gorgeous pillar of flame like to lead Moses to the promised land—only it's setting a trainload of live cattle on fire.

*(SCHWARZBERG looks suspiciously at the chandelier. It's lit, but dimly, as if at very low power. He shrugs, comes down off the ladder.)*

SCHWARZBERG: Tomorrow's gonna be sunshine. I'll get to work in the garden, finish the bride and the blind man.

TANYA: In the new Dance of Death.

SCHWARZBERG: American style. Very good, Mrs Vole.

TANYA: Thank you, Mister Schwarzberg.

SCHWARZBERG: It's all over, you know. That life. Today they run deisel electric, gas turbine—all hot shots. They never stop for water and they hit the junction at eighty miles per hour. Anyone tries to jump her, they'll end up cut to pieces under the wheels.

TANYA: The Vole Family Puppet Theater has also run aground in modern times. Leon and I were considering nailing our feet to the floor, becoming the Vole Fun Center. Kiddie rides, corn dogs. Save our money for a fiberglass carousel and a row of video pinball machines.

It's all fucked, you know. Rather badly.

(LITTLE JUNIOR *crosses outside. He stops, looking out toward the ocean. Sound of the sea.*)

(TANYA *calls to him.*)

TANYA: Little Junior!

LITTLE JUNIOR: Yeah?

TANYA: Come in and take off your clothes! I want to celebrate the end of the world. As we know it. Knew it.

(SCHWARZBERG *laughs.*)

LITTLE JUNIOR: *(Peering in window)* Who's that? Who said that?

(*The chandelier* SCHWARZBERG *has been repairing flickers.*)

(LITTLE JUNIOR *comes in. He looks around, sees* TANYA.)

(*The puppet theater, which has been standing idle, comes alive. First the devil [*NUNCLE*], now thin and lean, and then the* CROCODILE, *peer out of the puppet stage into the room.*)

TANYA: I'm sorry. I thought you were a ghost.

Someone I knew a long time ago.

(NUNCLE *and the* CROCODILE *bow.* LITTLE JUNIOR *doesn't move.*)

(*The chandelier flickers repeatedly.*)

(*Then* ISAIAH *is there.*)

(*Sound of someone weeping.*)

(LEON *steps out from behind the puppet booth. He takes a step toward* TANYA.)

(*Then* ROSE *is there.*)

(HELENA *is there.*)

(*Suddenly the light of the chandelier grows steady and brightens. The light is clean and clear, like afternoon sunshine.*)


## Scene Four

(*In the ballroom, everyone present*)

(*Crossfade: The Story of Cocount Joe, Part Three*)

ISAIAH: The story of Coconut Joe, Part Three.
It's a bright summer afternoon, and a middle-aged man can be seen walking along the Zatterre Degli Incurabili in the fabled city of Venice. There he goes.
The man on the Zattere is, of course, an American, a native of Kokomo, Indiana. He had planned to spend this day in the offices of Italo-Yugo Freight Forwarders, finalizing the transoceanic shipping of a thousand tons of Filipino coconut, currently in the hold of the *S S Calamari*, anchored at the Venetian docks.
However, Coconut Joe Iskowitz can't concentrate on business. His mind wanders, obsessed by the enigmatic Contessa Orsino, a woman he met on the quay the night before.

(*Night. A quay in Venice.* COCONUT JOE, *two* MASKED
VENETIANS, *the* CONTESSA ORSINO *in a black ballgown*)

COCONUT JOE: She stood there, distraught in the
moonlight.

CONTESSA: Oooooooooh….

MASKED VENETIAN 1: The Contessa Orsino is unable,
at this late hour, to find a boat to take her across the
Grand Canal.

MASKED VENETIAN 2: To the Palazzo Orsino.

MASKED VENETIAN 1: Share your gondola, Signore
Coconut Joe.

CONTESSA: *Grazie.*

COCONUT JOE: I'm sorry, I don't speak any…

CONTESSA: Thanks for the lift, Mister.

MASKED VENETIAN 2: They drift in the darkness. The
water slaps the gondola's black sides. A single candle
burns on its prow.

MASKED VENETIAN 1: The Contessa lights a Pall Mall.
They talk.

CONTESSA: I'm an American, though I've lived in
Venice for years. I'm married—to an Italian nobleman
of peculiar habits. He gives me diamonds, then strips
me, ties me to the bed, and beat me with his cane.

MASKED VENETIAN 1: The Contessa displays a bruise
on her upper arm.

CONTESSA: Look.

COCONUT JOE: That must hurt.

MASKED VENETIAN 1: And a bruise on her thigh.

CONTESSA: Look.

COCONUT JOE: That must hurt.

CONTESSA: It does. A lot. Kiss it.

MASKED VENETIAN 2: He does.

MASKED VENETIAN 1: To her enormous relief.

MASKED VENETIAN 2: They rock the gondola.

MASKED VENETIAN 1: For hours. Afterwards, the Contessa weeps.

MASKED VENETIAN 2: By the time they drift in alongside the dock of the Palazzo Orsino, Coconut Joe Iskowitz is madly, passionately in love.

*(Opera music.* COCONUT JOE, CONTESSA, FRIEDA*)*

ISAIAH: The very next night, Joe and the Contessa attend the Opera Della Saturno, along with her confidante, the enigmatic Frieda Mazowski, a Polish emigre.

COCONUT JOE: I'm an American, from Indiana. I...

FRIEDA: My father was a bandit from Moldavia, and my mother was a whore from Cracow. They're both dead, thank God.

CONTESSA: Shhhhh.

OPERA SINGERS: *(Singing operatically)*
*Dove posso trovare*
*Lautobus numero quattordice!*
*Ogni pensiero vola!*
*(Opera continuing under...)*

COCONUT JOE: My Italiano isn't very...

FRIEDA: That bishop and those three whores seek shelter from a thunderstorm and tell lies to keep the devil away.

ISAIAH: During the intermezzo, the Contessa asks Joe a favor.

CONTESSA: Joe, would you bring my husband a bottle of red wine. Lacryma Cristi. I hate him, but it's his birthday.

COCONUT JOE: I guess so. Sure.

(CONTESSA *hands* COCONUT JOE *the bottle of wine.*)

COCONUT JOE: Where is he?

CONTESSA: Count Orsino is in a monastic cell
maintained by the Cistercian Order of Nuns on an
island in the Venetian lagoon.

(ORSINO *appears in a monk's cell. He has a hunchback. A*
PROSTITUTE *is with him.* COCONUT JOE *approaches.*)

ORSINO: I am Orsino.
Life has swept me down horrible pathways of
misfortune. Now I have confined myself to this
island, dedicated to Christ and his holy sisters. I have
abandoned my palazzo, my paintings, left my beautiful
young wife...
On our wedding night I was overwhelmed by her
purity and unable to perform. She was frightened by
my body. I hated her. I stepped out of the bedroom
onto the terrace. I could hear my peacocks screaming
in the park. I went to see a prostitute who caressed my
hump and laughed.

PROSTITUTE: Fuck me, and your hump will melt away
like snow.

ORSINO: Get out, Sophia. The gentleman from America
and I have matters to discuss.

(PROSTITUTE *exits.*)

ORSINO: I, Count Girolamo Orsino, began to mistreat
my wife. She stabbed me with a jade letter opener.

(*Sound of weird erotic howling, rising in intensity*)

ORSINO: I whipped her and chained her in the dog
house. She howled in ecstasy. In that howling,
something inside me broke.

(*Howling fades to a pathetic, angry whimper.*)

ORSINO: Dragging in my hump the burden of my sins, I came here. The nuns gave me a cell.
Death will come for us, you and I. If you believe this grinning death is the end, you are wrong. If you believe it is the beginning, you are wrong. Mind and body have their end, and they exist eternally. We die, and we do not die.

COCONUT JOE: I guess so. Maybe.
I got a gift for you. From the Contessa.

ORSINO: I've been expecting it. I'm sure it's something—quite wonderful.

COCONUT JOE: It's just a bottle of Lacryma Christi. Red wine.

(ORSINO *opens the bottle, drinks.*)

COCONUT JOE: Happy birthday.

(ORSINO *laughs harshly, then doubles over in pain. He keeps laughing, until the pain and weakness overwhelm him.*)

ORSINO: My wife…has poisoned me.

ISAIAH: As he says these words, his eyes film over. He sees Venice for the last time, floating like a ghost city on the sea.

ORSINO: Arrrrghhh… *(He dies.)*

(NUNS *rush in.*)

NUN 1: He has murdered Orsino!

NUN 2: Carabinieri!

NUN 1: Police!

NUN 2: Call the Pope!

ISAIAH: Joe flees in a rowboat! Row row row your boat, gently down… *(Continuing under)*

COCONUT JOE: The Contessa. Got to find her. I love her. She'll help me. *(Chanting, in a panic)* Row row row your boat, gently down the stream… *(And continuing under…)*

ISAIAH: The Rio Nuovo, along the Guidecca, into the Grand Canal.

MASKED VENETIAN 1: The bells of Saint Mark's! Ding ding ding ding… *(And on under)*

MASKED VENETIAN 2: The island of Venice is shrouded in unusual gloom. It seems to float on the lagoon, drifting ever so slowly toward the open sea, a journey of a thousand years.

COCONUT JOE: Ah, the Contessa's gondola! A lantern swinging from the prow. It looks empty…

ISAIAH: Joe rows closer. In the bottom of the gondola, two naked bodies intertwined, making love. The Contessa Orsino and Frieda Mazowski.
The Contessa sees the desperate, confused face of Coconut Joe.
She untangles herself.

CONTESSA: Your love for me has made you a liar, a poisoner, and a fugitive. It has destroyed your life. In this knowledge, Mister Coconut Joe Iskowitz—despair—and die.

*(The CONTESSA takes out a pistol, points it at COCONUT JOE. FRIEDA laughs.)*

CONTESSA: Who could blame me for killing the man who poisoned my husband!

*(BANG!!)*

FRIEDA: Stupid bitch. You missed him. Give me that gun!

*(FRIEDA grabs the gun and blasts away. BANG! BANG! BANG! BANG!)*

COCONUT JOE: Missed me!

CONTESSA: Police! Police! A murderer!

ISAIAH: Joe rows like a madman along the docks of Venice.

COCONUT JOE: *(Chanting fast, in a panic)* Row row row your boat, gently down the stream, merrily merrily merrily merrily merrily...

ISAIAH: Finally he sees what he's looking for. The *S S Calamari*! He climbs on, scrambles down into the hold. He burrows into the piles of coconut, tossing it over his head, burying himself in the hot, damp whiteness.

*(Sound of ship's foghorn)*

ISAIAH: The *S S Calamari* sets sail for America.

*(Sound of the ocean. Gulls)*

ISAIAH: At sea. Tartar sailors play cards on deck.

TARTAR SAILOR: Go fish!

ISAIAH: Down in the hold, Joe is pillowed on tons of white flake.
He tastes...

COCONUT JOE: This coconut's not Zamboanga Angel Food. It's Grade D Filipino. And it's rotten!
Damn that Baron Dramer. This stuff is decomposing. It stinks. The fumes are making me dizzy...
Help!

ISAIAH: On deck, the Tartars hear his cries. They believe there's an evil spirit in the hold.

TARTARS: Volokolamski! Moshiaska!

COCONUT JOE: HELP! HELLLLP!

ISAIAH: They double lock the hatches.
Joe stays alive somehow, eating nothing but rotten coconut. Forty-seven days in hell, at a hundred and twenty degrees.

COCONUT JOE: *(Delirious, sings)*
Buzzing of the trees and the cigarette bees
In the crystal whiskey fountain
Lemonade sings of the buzzard wings
In the Big Cock Randy Mountain
There's a puddle of glue and a da da dee
You can paddle all around em in a big canee...
Oh my God! This coconut's gotten wet. Salt water!

ISAIAH: The hatch opens. Sailors grab Joe and haul him
on deck. The Captain is a Greek from Smyrna. Nikos
something or other.

CAPTAIN NIKOS: Just call me Captain Nik-Nik. I have
bad news. We've sprung a leak, and the crew think
you're a Jonah.

COCONUT JOE: That's ridiculous. I'm actually the
shipper of the cargo—the coconut. I had to run from
the Italian police. I...

CAPTAIN NIKOS: You might as well shut up. None of
them speak English.

TARTARS: Volokolamski! Moshaiska!

CAPTAIN NIKOS: You're going overboard.

ISAIAH: But at that moment...

PIRATES: Yo ho! Yo ho! Yo ho! WHOOOO! HOOOOO!

*(Sound of cannonfire, swords clashing!)*

ISAIAH: A pirate ship attacks the *S S Calamari*. The
pirate captain is a ruthless and bloodthirsty woman!

PIRATE QUEEN: Board the bastards! Cut their nuts off!

*(Cannon! Groans! Splashes! BOOM! BADABOOM!)*

ISAIAH: The *S S Calamari* explodes.

*(BOOM!)*

ISAIAH: Another explosion rocks the pirate ship. Both
ships sink into the lowland sea.

Coconut Joe grabs a floating door and climbs aboard.

COCONUT JOE: Everyone else is drowned. I'm the only one saved. Thank God. There is some justice in this crazy...

ISAIAH: Before he could finish the thought, the bloodthirsty pirate queen hauls herself out of the sea and climbs aboard his door.

PIRATE QUEEN: Plenty of room.

ISAIAH: The ocean is calm and empty. The sun is high. Coconut Joe and the pirate queen look at each other.

*(Long silence between them. Sound of the sea)*

COCONUT JOE: Don't I know you from somewhere?

ISAIAH: The pirate queen doesn't answer. They drift on, over the wide ocean...

*(Crossfade back to Hotel Splendide ballroom)*


## Scene Five

*(The ballroom, midafternoon)*

*(Everyone's there.)*

LEON: Thank you all for gathering together to hear what I have to say. Tanya has cut the phone lines to insure that we won't be disturbed. It's extremely simple.
We have tried to avoid bloodshed. We've used our skill, our art, and our considerable talents. We have been met with lies. Lies, Mister Sandoval.

*(LEON takes out a pistol. He aims it at ISAIAH.)*

LEON: This is a .45 automatic. It can blow a hole through a motor block, and it's pointing at your midsection. So, Isaiah Sandoval, let's talk. Let's talk about a charitable contribution. Give all your money to the Vole Family Puppet Theater. Then Tanya, myself, and all our little friends will disappear. Into thin air. And you will still be here, at the Hotel Splendide, safe and sound.

ISAIAH: Who told you I had money?

LEON: Our mutual friend. Eddie. He'd seen it. A red plastic suitcase, like a child's, full of hundred-dollar bills.

ROSE: Eddie's a sicko. Don't you get it? He told you a story.

LEON: The boy was upset that Mister Sandoval threatened him—with a pistol. He confided in us. Now.
Give us the money. Or I will start shooting people. Rose first, and then these others. Then I'll shoot you.

ISAIAH: There is no money.

LEON: That's a pity then. All these people are going to die.

ROSE: Isaiah doesn't have two dimes to rub…

TANYA: Shut up!

(TANYA *slaps* ROSE *hard across the face.* ROSE *tumbles to the floor from the force of the blow, but she's more surprised than seriously hurt.*)

ROSE: You don't know Eddie like I do.

TANYA: I told you to…

ROSE: He'd say anything to fuck me up.

LEON: This is a waste of time.
Behold! The shepherd Acis, kissing the sandals, the thighs, the lips of the nymph Galatea—while the fife of one-eyed Polyphemus already sounds close at hand— if he could only hear it.

Isaiah, you don't want another death to your credit.
Like your wife. There she lay on the front seat, her
silver skin laced with her golden blood.
We'll lay Rose right alongside her.

(ISAIAH *doesn't speak. The* CROCODILE *puppet appears
suddenly on* LEON's *free hand. Its snout slowly turns
toward* ROSE, *along with the gun.)*

LEON: *(In* CROCODILE's *voice)* Goodbye, Rose.
See you next time around.

(ISAIAH *steps in front of* ROSE, *shielding her with his body.*
LEON *takes careful aim. He clicks the hammer back.)*

(BANG!! LEON's *gun drops to the floor, and he screams,
clutching his leg. Blood.* HELENA *has shot him with a small
revolver.)*

HELENA: I wouldn't let that clown shoot you, baby. Not
in my hotel.

(LEON *grimaces with pain.* TANYA *breaks into tears. Her
sobbing shakes her whole body. Finally,* HELENA *approaches
her.)*

HELENA: It's a leg wound. You gonna take care of him,
or do I have to do that too?
I'd call a doctor, but some bitch has ripped out the
phones.

*(One of the wires holding up the huge overhead chandelier
suddenly snaps. With a great tinkling of crystal, the mass
of glass and metal swings down, back and forth, blinking on
and off. At last it hangs on one frayed wire.)*

*(Light on all of them changes, as if they're in a dream.* LEON
*moans. A thousand fragments of light from the crystals
shimmer over them.)*

SCHWARZBERG: Nooze, Nooze or Mirra, Nooze. Get
your Nooze. Nooze or Mirra. Nooze...

*(End Part One)*

## PART TWO
### In The Garden—Twilight
### Scene One

*(In the garden)*

*(Green buds are out on the early plants, even a flower or two.* SCHWARZBERG *is up on the ladder. He lowers the final dropcloth off his painting on the garden wall. The drop was covering a blind man, being led by a dancing skeleton down a country road. A big tractor-trailer comes at them around a curve. Other figures have been completed—a bride at the altar, a gambler holding four aces—each accompanied by a dancing, grinning skeleton.)*

*(The American Dance of Death is still fragmentary, some figures half painted, a few only sketched, but the plan of the whole can be seen. It's a wonderful work of art, somehow joyful despite its chilling scenario.)*

*(*HELENA *sits in a chair, with a drink.)*

HELENA: *(Sings)*
Once upon a time, a duck drank wine
The monkey played the fiddle
On a streetcar line
The streetcar broke, the monkey choke
Trying to get to heaven on a billy goat…

*(*SCHWARZBERG *comes down from the ladder, gets himself a drink from a tray. He sits down near* HELENA.*)*

SCHWARZBERG: Self-service today, I see.

HELENA: Little Junior's down on the rocks with Isaiah. Probably boring him to death with little sea creatures. They both need the company.

SCHWARZBERG: I thought of something. Wouldn't it be funny if there really was a red plastic suitcase, full of beautiful money, and Isaiah was just too damn stubborn to give it up.

HELENA: There isn't. You think I'd shoot someone if I didn't know what I was doing? First rule of hotel management. People don't pay you for six months, you're entitled to go through their stuff. Nothing but notebooks full of words, old photographs. Rose owns three T-shirts, and some ten-dollar earrings.

SCHWARZBERG: Would've been funny, that's all. I saw Mister Leon Vole. He's limping around.

HELENA: He should be by now.

SCHWARZBERG: I saw them breaking down the theater, covering the rat cage. On their way. Getting on at Zerega Avenue, down to Cathedral Parkway, Delancey Street, to South Ferry and over the sea.

(HELENA *stands, looks over the painting on the garden wall.*)

HELENA: Mister Schwarzberg, this is pretty impressive, but are you sure it'll draw tourists? People don't like to be reminded of their mortality, especially on vacation.

SCHWARZBERG: They'll love it. That little frisson.

HELENA: I still can't see serving breakfast among the boney company.

SCHWARZBERG: Hey, it's a *great* work of art.

HELENA: I know. With a message.

SCHWARZBERG: Carpe diem, darling. Golden girls and boys all must, like chimney sweepers, come to dust.

HELENA: Mister Whelk won't like it.

SCHWARZBERG: Fuck Mister Whelk. It's you and me, babe.

HELENA: We'll see.

(*Long silence.* HELENA *looks at the painting again.*)

HELENA: That Mister Vole—an extraordinary man.
He'd steal the butter off a blind man's bread and put
him on the wrong road home.

## Scene Two

*(By the sea)*

*(Sound of the sea.* ISAIAH *and* LITTLE JUNIOR *alone.)*

ISAIAH: You're right, Little Junior. Being down by
the ocean is good for me. I feel better—cleaner and
stronger.

LITTLE JUNIOR: You see.
Hey—look at that gull.

ISAIAH: In fact, I'm going to appoint you my personal
physician. Doctor Little Junior.

LITTLE JUNIOR: Just skimming the waves. That's where
they like to fly the best. Right between heaven and
earth.

ISAIAH: It's gray out there, almost white—a soft,
glowing white. Air and water the same color. The
horizon could be anywhere. *(Sings)*
There's a beautiful light on the ocean
There's a beautiful light on the sea
Beautiful light on the ocean
Where my darling lies waiting for me...
Little Junior, you know what it means to be a human
being? It means that you have to have more mercy than
God.

*(Sound of the sea)*

LITTLE JUNIOR: Let's get back, O K? I want to see Rose.

*(*ISAIAH *laughs.)*

*(The Chinese lanterns flicker, and the hotel garden is around
them.)*

## Scene Three

*(Back in the garden)*

*(*ROSE *is there. She sits close to* LITTLE JUNIOR. ISAIAH *talks to them.)*

ISAIAH: This world is a hard place for me, Rosie. All the coming and going. The faces of people we loved only yesterday vanish into the smoky twilight. Here and gone.

But we live on, don't we?

*(He laughs quietly to himself.)*

Telling stories as the sun goes down. Coconut Joe. I'll tell you the end, Rose. You and Little Junior. Tell it to the starfish in the tide pools. Tell it to each other, under the covers. Tell it to your children.

*(Crossfade: The Story of Coconut Joe, Part Four)*

ISAIAH: The story of Coconut Joe, Part Four. Remember… The bloodthirsty Pirate Queen and Coconut Joe float on a door, in an endless tropical sea…

COCONUT JOE: Don't I know you from somewhere?

*(A long silence)*

COCONUT JOE: I recognize you. You're Ava, from Berlin. You rescued me from the canal.

AVA: You're that jerk, Coconut Joe Iskowitz, who thought I was Baron Dramer's daughter. Dramer and Krumm, that cookie man, were ripping off Universal Bake Shoppe. You were there to get blamed. And killed.

COCONUT JOE: Those no-good bastards. I'd like to find them and…

AVA: It doesn't matter.

I used to fuck people and they'd pay me. Now I slit
their throats and take the money. No difference. Both
activities are equally ugly and pointless.

COCONUT JOE: I was a coconut buyer. I guess I don't
even have a job anymore. And my little daughter...
what'll she do without me?

AVA: I was a hooker with a tender spot for jerks from
Kokomo. Now I'm a pirate queen. Without a ship.
That's fate, I guess.
Do you want to make love to me?

COCONUT JOE: Once I did, alongside that canal. After
seeing you kill all those people—and on this little door
in the ocean—I'm not sure I could...

AVA: Just shut up.

ISAIAH: They drift...
For seven days they lie together in the burning sun and
starve. They don't speak. Toward evening, when the
heat of the day breaks, they look, for a moment, into
each other's eyes.
On the morning of the eighth day, their door washes
up on the shore of a tropical island.

*(Tropical island.* ISLANDERS *chant as* COCONUT JOE *and*
AVA *stagger ashore.)*

ISLANDERS: *(Chanting)*
Hokum, pokum, elecampane
Icum spikum Spinto Spain
Ekee-okee adama pokee
Nokum smokum alicum skee
Hixum naxum
Prixum praxum
Hokum pokum France and Spain
Round the world and back again!

*(The* ISLANDERS *give them food and water. They eat and
drink.)*

COCONUT JOE: *(With mouth full)* You saved us! You saved our lives!

AVA: Thanks, I guess.

COCONUT JOE: Who are you?

ISLANDER 1: We are wild uncivilized natives from the far side of Loon Island.

AVA: No kidding. What do you do all day?

ISLANDER 1: Fish.

ISLANDER 2: Sing.

ISLANDERS: *(Chanting softly)* Hokum pokum elecampane… *(Continuing under)*

AVA: I like these guys, and I think, with a little work, I can become their queen.

ISLANDER 1: Goodbye.

*(The ISLANDERS begin to exit.)*

AVA: Hey! Wait for me.

*(They not only do so, but pick up the door, putting AVA on it. As they begin to carry her off, she turns back toward COCONUT JOE.)*

AVA: Come see me sometime, Mister Coconut Joe. Please.

COCONUT JOE: I will.

*(AVA and the ISLANDERS exit, chanting.)*

AVA & ISLANDERS:
Hokum, pokum, elecampane
Icum spikum Spinto Spain…

*(They're gone.)*

ISAIAH: Once again, Joe's alone. He looks down at his feet.

COCONUT JOE: Somebody's wallet, lying in the sand. Hmmm. This I D card says Mister Silvio Whelk, Owner, Loon Island Hotel.

ISAIAH: The Loon Island Hotel, a decaying wreck of a once-grand building on the beach. Balconies… chandeliers…a garden.

*(The impressive* MR WHELK *appears, an aging sophisticate in a frayed white linen suit. With him, a beautiful young woman in a sort of sarong,* DIEUDONNE.*)*

MR WHELK: I'm Whelk. What's your game?

COCONUT JOE: I'm Coconut Joe. I found your wallet, and I want to give it back.

MR WHELK: How do you like that for an honest man? Honest as the day is…

DIEDONNE: Long. The day is long.

MR WHELK: Dieudonne, give him a reward.

DIEDONNE: He returned a fat wallet. That sort of stupidity shouldn't be encouraged.

MR WHELK: Give him a hundred.

*(*DIEUDONNE *does so reluctantly.)*

COCONUT JOE: Thanks, Mister Whelk. I appreciate it.

MR WHELK: Don't appreciate it too much, my friend. There's nothing to buy on Loon Island. Besides, I can spare it. Business has been good lately.

COCONUT JOE: I gotta admit I'm surprised to hear that, Mister Whelk. This hotel is a wreck.

MR WHELK: The hotel business is for shit. Loon Island is rather far off the usual tourist routes. In fact, you're our first visitor in…

DIEDONNE: Ages. Eons.

MR WHELK: I was referring to the candy business. I'm a confectioner. We manufacture Loon Island rock candy in the basement of this very hotel. The island population is addicted.
Dieudonne, do we have any work at the sugar vat?

DIEDONNE: Not at the moment.

MR WHELK: That's a pity. That's really …

DIEDONNE: Unfortunate.

MR WHELK: Fire someone. Fire Haleloke. I don't give a shit. Joseph Iskowitz, I believe I see for you a window of opportunity. It knocks.

COCONUT JOE: What?

MR WHELK: The window.

DIEDONNE: It knocks. Follow me.

COCONUT JOE: Mister Whelk, before I go, there are a few ideas about candy and coconut I'd like to share with you. You got coconut palms on this island. Joe Iskowitz has been in the business for years, and I've learned a trick or two.

MR WHELK: *(Laughs)* We can't put this man on the sugar vat, Dieudonne. He's an original thinker. I need an assistant manager. He'll do.

(DIEUDONNE *leads* COCONUT JOE *off, and he immediately reappears, in a white linen suit exactly like* MR WHELK's. MR WHELK *himself is gone.* DIEUDONNE *reappears nearby.*)

COCONUT JOE: I have become the assistant manager of the Rock Candy Factory here on Loon Island—Assistant Manager Joe.
Loon Island has no communication with the rest of the world, if the rest of the world is still out there.
Once a week I go to dinner with Mister Whelk.

*(A Chopin piano sonata plays.)*

COCONUT JOE: After dinner, Dieudonne plays Chopin
on an old upright. We consume huge quantities of
cheap brandy.

Last night after dinner, Mister Whelk took me aside.

Mister Whelk: Joe, when you think of your friend
Silvio, have pity in your heart. I'd give everybody a
drink if I had enough liquor. I'd give everybody love, if
I had some.

Dieudonne and I leave tomorrow. For Bimini. You'll be
in charge here.

DIEDONNE: Bye-bye, Assistant Manager Joe. Good luck.

*(End Chopin sonata.)*

COCONUT JOE: When I woke the following afternoon,
with a splitting headache, they were both gone. I don't
know how they left the island. I never heard from them
or saw them again.

ISAIAH: Coconut Joe runs the rock candy factory on
Loon Island, far from everything he's ever known. He
thinks now and then about trying to find Ava on the
other side of the island—but somehow he doesn't go.
He shows the natives new uses for their coconut crop.
And, strangely enough, Joe becomes a sort of doctor.
His honesty, sweetness, and even his simple touch
seem to help the sick and troubled. He discovers a
power within him, and when he calls on it with all his
soul it can give comfort, or even heal.

Two years later, one of the islanders tells Joe that Ava,
the pirate queen, who was living alone on the far side
of the island, killed herself. She slit her wrists, and bled
to death into the sand.

Years pass. Coconut Joe is the leader of the island,
responsible for everyone's happiness. The people love
him.

Once a week he goes to the other side of the island and
puts flowers on Ava's grave.

*(As he does so, chanting)*

ISLANDERS: *(Solemnly)*
Hokum, pokum, elecampane
Icum spikum Spinto Spain
Ekee-okee adama pokee
Nokum smokum alicum skee.

ISAIAH: Coconut Joe sometimes wanders down to the
old wooden dock at the foot of the Loon Island Hotel.
He goes out to the end of it and looks at the sea.

*(Sound of the sea)*

ISAIAH: Kokomo, Indiana, his daughter, the Universal
Bake Shoppe, all these are distant memories, without
vividness or pain. He has lost all hope of return.
Time passes. A sunset. A sunrise. A sunset.

COCONUT JOE: I'm sitting here on this rotting pier, over
the dark blue of the lagoon. I'm trying to think. I'm
trying to understand everything that's happened to
me. I'm trying to get hold of myself. It's night, the vast
night of this warm tropic sea without end. A million
stars are in the sky.
Somewhere among them she is waiting for me.

*(The cry of birds)*

COCONUT JOE & ISAIAH: Dawn. Birds cry at the world's
end. The sky is white, and against that white, a sail.

ISAIAH: A boat glides into the lagoon, smooth as glass.
A teenager stands in the prow, browned by the sun,
her eyes the blue-green of the sea.
The girl is Coconut Joe's daughter, now seventeen,
who has been searching the world for him. She's found
him at last. They know each other in a moment, despite
the years. She cries out…

DAUGHTER: Daddy…

ISAIAH: But Coconut Joe is unable to answer. A great sadness overwhelms him. He lay down on the end of the pier, in this strange land, under the hot sun, and it seemed to him that he was melting away. His daughter took him in her arms, and Coconut Joe Iskowitz cried like a baby.

*(Weeping. Silence)*

ISAIAH: After a long while, they talked. They told each other everything.

COCONUT JOE: Whats it like now, back home?

DAUGHTER: It's winter, Dad. The cold wind still blows across the river from the north. But by the time we get there, it might be the very beginning of spring.

COCONUT JOE: What happened to Universal Bake Shoppe?

DAUGHTER: They're all in jail, Dad. The company's gone. There's a city housing project there now.

COCONUT JOE: Well—I guess we'll start over.

DAUGHTER: I guess we will.

COCONUT JOE: *(Sings)*
Oh, the humming of the bees in the cigarette trees
Beside the crystal fountain

*(COCONUT JOE's DAUGHTER joins in the song.)*

COCONUT JOE & DAUGHTER: *(Sing)*
Come with me, and we'll go see
The Big Rock Candy Mountain!

*(Crossfade back to Hotel Splendide garden)*

## Scene Four

*(In the garden at last)*

*(*HELENA, ISAIAH, LEON, LITTLE JUNIOR, ROSE, SCHWARZBERG, *and* TANYA*)*

*(The* VOLES *are about to leave. They're dressed for travel. The puppet theater is broken down and packed up to go.)*

TANYA: Our booking agent has advised us of some excellent opportunities in another part of the world. We like to travel. Weve slept in the puppet booth too many times to mention. The bed from *The Princess and the Pea* makes a lovely pillow, and Leon covers me with his coat.

*(Silence)*

LEON: I'd appreciate the return of my gun. Unloaded, of course.

ISAIAH: It's in the sea.

TANYA: I don't suppose it would mean anything to mention that you met us at a rather low point in our career.

LEON: Tanya, please.

TANYA: Thank you for your…kindness.

*(Silence, as* LEON *looks them all over.)*

LEON: When you die, I'm sure you'll meet a lot of people I know. They're all in hell. I want you to give them my greetings, and say that I hope the eternal torments aren't too hard on them.
This whole fucking world is a crime.
The hour is struck. The Vole Family Theater exits.

*(*LEON *takes the slightest bow. Whether he does so mockingly, or sincerely, it is impossible to tell.)*

*(Instead of applause, silence)*

TANYA: The walk to the bus station in town shouldn't
be too bad in this weather.
Little Junior, would you be kind enough to help us
down to the road. Leon's leg is still painful. Boris's
cage, and the theatre, are more than we can manage
easily.

*(No one moves.)*

HELENA: Get out.

*(Struggling with their paraphernalia, they manage it
between them.)*

LEON: Behold! One-eyed Polyphemus and his Galatea,
on their way. He will love her forever, and the fife of
the damned cyclops will haunt you all.

*(LEON exits. When she reaches the door, TANYA turns back
to the group.)*

TANYA: Leon's a gambler and a thief. I'm a whore.
We'll survive. *(She exits.)*

*(Sound of the sea. The cries of birds)*

*(SCHWARZBERG gets busy, closing paint cans, putting
brushes away, folding up his ladder. He turns on the Chinese
lanterns.)*

SCHWARZBERG: Nooze or Mirra, Nooze. Nooze or
Mirra, Nooze. Get ya paper, early edition. Nooze,
Nooze, Nooze or Mirra.

*(LITTLE JUNIOR and ROSE sit together.)*

*(HELENA sits by ISAIAH. He lies back in the chaise, facing
away from the audience. He lights a cigarette.)*

ISAIAH: Where's Coconut Joe? Just a pile of husks
against a concrete wall…
The autumn wind has risen in the east. When it passes,
without a memory, this worthless body becomes a
dream…

HELENA: Shhh, baby. Enough. One world at a time,
O K?

You're here in my garden, in the beautiful Hotel
Splendide.

*(Silence)*

LITTLE JUNIOR: You know, Mister S, I think I want a
tattoo.

SCHWARZBERG: You getting one just cause I gave one to
Rose?

LITTLE JUNIOR: No. I want something like you're
painting on the wall. A skeleton. Small one.

SCHWARZBERG: You don't want one of those. The
girls are gonna think you're a motorcycle jerk, or just
morbid. How about a sea creature? I do a nice starfish.
Or a flower? You see what Rose got? She got a rose.

LITTLE JUNIOR: Maybe I'll get a…

SCHWARZBERG: Think about it. Take a walk with Rose.
Down on the rocks. Stick your feet in a tide pool.
I'll be here when you get back. I ain't going nowhere.

HELENA: You can go, Rose. I'll keep an eye on Isaiah.

ISAIAH: Nobody's got to keep an eye on me.

HELENA: Go ahead. Go.

*(ROSE and LITTLE JUNIOR exit through the arched garden
doorway. They're gone.)*

*(Sound of the sea)*

## Scene Five

*(In the garden, twilight)*

*(HELENA sits near ISAIAH. SCHWARZBERG brings her
a drink, takes one himself. ISAIAH leans back, smokes.*

SCHWARZBERG *takes a long look around the wall at his painting.)*

HELENA: Well, Mister S, when you gonna finish the garden wall? I wanna see the completed masterpiece.

*(*SCHWARZBERG *laughs suddenly. He turns to* HELENA.*)*

SCHWARZBERG: Finish? Masterpieces take time, Helena. I'm in no hurry. You know why the skeletons are dancing? It's their secret. There is no death. It's a show. We live forever.

HELENA: Well, then. I guess we've got all the time in the world.

*(Silence)*

*(Sound of the sea)*

ISAIAH: In the beginning, the Hotel Splendide was built in the chaos of ice and the polar... No. Take it downtown, on Azalea Avenue, by the sea. *(Sings)* By the sea, by the sea, by the beautiful sea...
A single raindrop ripples the dead canal, sets the black boat rocking. Pall Malls spilled over the red plush seat. The lantern sways, and the shadows dance.
Sail away, sail away...
A cigarette is burning. Smoke rises from a green glass ashtray. Green glass ashtray, smoke sails up into the light.
Wait here, right here. And we'll begin.
Now.

### END OF PLAY